THE OTHER SIDE
OF THIS LIFE

The Other Side of This Life

TED ROBB

LUMINARE PRESS
WWW.LUMINAREPRESS.COM

Printed in the United States of America

Luminare Press
442 Charnelton St.
Eugene, OR 97401
www.luminarepress.com

LCCN: 2021920214
ISBN: 978-1-64388-782-1

To my children,
David, Felicia, and Greg,
For their faithful love and support

ۈ

Author's Note

Writing a memoir is like merging multiple photos into a single portrait. But for this exercise, I would have considered the picture of my life as very bland indeed. It has taken me years to act upon the idea of telling my story, and I have spent the entirety of the COVID-19 pandemic dusting off memories and arranging the pictures they conjure on paper. I've done my best to accurately portray the players and scenes of my life as I remember them and, in some cases, consulted with others who shared in certain stories.

Throughout the drafting process, I have come to realize my life can be divided into three parts. Act One includes my childhood, formative years, marriage, and my children's early years. Act Two covers my years in politics, roughly a span of twelve years in which opportunities and acquaintances very much changed the trajectory of my professional life. Act Three starts in Philadelphia, when at age forty, I left the political sector to focus on the nonprofit work that I hope will define my legacy. As I am now in my eighth decade, it is interesting that Act Three begins half a lifetime ago, but that is how I see my story.

I'd like to thank Carrie Hagen, Cynthia Ryan, and Ellie Robb for their research, drafting, and editing assistance. The title of this book, *The Other Side of This Life*, comes from the Jefferson Airplane song of the same name. The band's antiwar music first appealed to me over fifty years ago, and this song's lyrics speak to the spirit behind many of my otherwise inexplicable choices.

> *Would you like to know a secret*
> *just between you and me*
>
> *I don't know where I'm going next,*
> *I don't know who I'm gonna be*
>
> *But that's the other side of this life*
> *I've been leading*
>
> *That's the other side of this life.*

Reflecting on my life has given me both fortitude and hope as the world has shut down. Had COVID-19 not arrived, forcing me inward, I think I may have fallen into the trap of so many people who say they are going to do something like write a book but never get around to it. Penning this narrative has given me a purpose, a final product to work toward. It has anchored me.

Being homebound also has allowed me to rethink how I prioritize people and time. Until a year ago, I had never had a weekly phone call with my children and grandchildren. Now we speak over Zoom every Wednesday night. I love hearing the kids share their memories of their mother, and I'm shocked at what they remember about their childhoods. There are so many things I've forgotten about their upbringing. Participating as an active listener excites me.

My daughter, Felicia, tells me that if my dear wife, Peg, were alive, I would jolly well be telephoning all kinds of people from the past. She has had a ball calling friends and family she hasn't heard from in years. "Get on the phone!" she says to me. She has her mother's spark.

I'm happy to hear from people, but I hesitate to follow her example. I think it's because for so long, I've seen such interactions as needing to have a purpose. I don't have a problem picking up the phone to call a Yale classmate in an effort to raise funds. But now I think, "A lot of guys don't have anybody to talk to. While I still have my faculties, I should ring and say, 'How are you doing?'" Isn't that purpose enough? To check in with someone with whom you have a valued, shared past? Certainly that's more worthwhile than only interacting with one's memories. Memories are both wonderful and dangerous. It wouldn't be hard at all to spend every one of my evenings in the basement, alone with my pipe, my whiskey and my television, and let film after film transport me through time. It will be difficult to find the wherewithal to reengage with society after COVID immunizations lift pandemic protocols. Then I'm going to have to force myself to interact outside of my home. Perhaps if it wasn't for my family phone calls, I'd almost have forgotten how to be civil.

Keeping up with current events throughout quarantine certainly stretched my sense of civility. The pandemic gave most of us too much time to watch the political cloud that loomed over America prior to Joe Biden's election. It seemed to grow heavier and darker every day, threatening most of those I've spent my professional life trying to help: the poor, the elderly, the marginalized. It's still there, I know, just a little farther off in the sky, gathering strength for a stand another few years from now.

Ironically, the houses that we want so desperately to escape have given us a false feeling of safety. Increasingly distanced from one another, we've tuned in only to the voices that make us feel like the cloud can't touch us. But, of course, it has. This has been such a long, dark season that, until the cloud began to weaken, I don't think I realized the power it had over my body. The day after Joe Biden's inauguration, I felt a release in my muscles. As I slept, relief had started to settle in.

I'm so pleased that I participated in the 2020 election. The day before Election Day, I made my way to City Hall to cast my ballot early. The National Guard had encircled the building, prepared to engage rioters who the press had anticipated would arrive. I didn't know what to expect, but I didn't want to wait in long, crowded lines during the pandemic on Election Day. I would have risked it, though, if it was necessary to cast my vote. I had no problem at all approaching the right office and asking someone to help me navigate the process. It was easy. I was so pleased that I did that.

"Ted," I said to myself, "you did the right thing here."

Despite the nation's fears, the election passed rather quietly. Then in early January, the president of the United States refused to accept defeat, instigated a riot, and we watched in horror as American citizens stormed the Capitol building.

On inauguration morning, I watched the ceremony with a book in my hand. My attention moved between the book and the television screen as Senator Amy Klobuchar moderated a respectful service of speeches and songs in front of a rather empty lawn at the Capitol. And then a voice captured my attention. It belonged to Amanda Gorman, a Harvard graduate and the nation's first youth poet-laureate. As she read the words to her poem "The Hill We Climb," tears spilled from my eyes.

"When day comes we ask ourselves,

Where can we find light in this never-ending shade?

The loss we carry,

A sea we must wade

We've braved the belly of the beast

We've learned that quiet isn't always peace

And the norms and notions

of what just is

Isn't always just-ice

And yet the dawn is ours

before we knew it

Somehow we do it

Somehow we've weathered and witnessed

a nation that isn't broken

but simply unfinished…"

I just fell apart as she spoke, the poetry cascading from her lips through the screen.

Yes, Amanda Gorman. You've stated it perfectly.

"Somehow we've weathered and witnessed a nation that isn't broken but simply unfinished."

ACT ONE

‑‑‑

"She lacks everything that makes living easy, she possesses most things that make it worthwhile."

—EDNA FISCHEL GELLHORN

❖ 1 ❖

My life began the moment I stepped onto a train heading west.

I remember going to Grand Central Station late one summer when I was nine years old. Mother and my governess, Mal, accompanied me to a platform, where an Amtrak conductor greeted us. Mother put me and my suitcase on the train and waved good-bye. I wouldn't see her for a year.

I had never gone anywhere by myself before. And I had rarely left Mal's side. Every second of my young life had been controlled and managed. Mal had chosen my clothes, dressed me, seen to my hygiene, and escorted me everywhere. Outside of sleeping, I had never had a moment alone. Now I would travel to Chicago and stay overnight in my first hotel. The following day, two adult chaperones would guide me and about a dozen other boys to a boarding school in Tucson, Arizona. There I would live for three years.

Most children in my position would have been terrified. I felt ecstatic. I felt free! Somehow I knew that this was the best thing that could happen to me. I followed the conductor up and down the aisle as he checked and clicked tickets. I wanted to be just like him when I grew up. Nothing seemed more exciting.

I assume Mother watched the train pull away, but I don't know what she thought or felt. I'm also not sure if either of us realized I would never really live with her again. From that moment on, other than returning to Park Avenue for summer holidays, I would take care of myself.

During the three-day journey to Tucson, I thought I was in heaven. I loved looking out the train window at the changing landscapes, and eating meals and bunking in the sleeper car. I felt like I was living in a dream sequence. I had no idea what to expect in Arizona, but I knew life would be very different. I couldn't have been happier.

❖ 2 ❖

U p until I went west, I lived in New York City with Mother at 1040 Park Avenue on 86th Street. Dad had lived with us in Manhattan during the first year of my life, but just after my first birthday—May 25, 1934—my parents decided to divorce after four years of marriage. Dad, forty, moved to Connecticut, and Mother, twenty-eight, soon hired Malvine de Coninck, a live-in Belgian nanny in her midforties. It was Mal who would have the strongest adult influence on my childhood.

Although I have no doubt that Mother loved me, I knew from a very young age that she wasn't very interested in traditional motherhood. All of my time with her in those days resembled pony shows. Young, beautiful, and wealthy, Mother loved hosting cocktail parties. At some point during those evenings, she would beckon, and Mal would parade me—"little Teddy"—around the room. I would talk nicely to all of her friends, and then Mal and I would disappear.

Mother and Mal got along extremely well, and I just adored my governess. We spent long mornings and afternoons walking in Central Park between 59th and 79th streets on Fifth Avenue. There I would play with children watched by Mal and her nanny friends. A fervent Catholic, Mal was the one who also took me to St. Jean Baptiste's on 76th and Lexington. My great grandfather, Thomas Fortune Ryan, had donated the money to build the Italian Renaissance Revival church, and Mal made sure that I took great pride in it. The majesty of the building's interior, particularly that of the altar, took my breath away. I never minded going to Mass. I came to associate the beauty of the church with serenity. It was also one of the few places where I didn't feel lonely. I think this is largely due to a lesson I learned in catechism class. I can very clearly remember a teacher telling me that I had a guardian angel dedicated just to me. My heart leaped when I heard this. It captured my faith. I started talking to my guardian angel as a lonely little boy, and occasionally I still do. As I get older, I take great comfort in knowing that an angel watches over me.

I doubt, however, that my angel watched me more closely than Malvine de Coninck. Her attention could be stifling, but I certainly needed her. She was the closest thing I had to an involved family member.

I can't say that I saw Mal as a parent; at the same time, I understood that she functioned as one. Neither Mother nor Dad, for example, showed much physical affection. I never felt that Mother placed me above other parts of her life. But with Mal I never starved for attention. I knew that I was her first priority. Mal was very strict and did, at times, seem like a paid jailer. She always made sure that wherever I went, I was dressed to the nines and behaved like a proper little gentleman.

Mal's role in my life was the type of thing I wished I could discuss with a sibling. I did have three older half-siblings, but they lived far away, and I didn't know them very well. More than anything else, I wanted a brother or sister like all my cousins had. They all seemed happy in their traditional family units, and I envied their companionship. What I would have given for someone about my age with whom I could share ideas and experiences! There was so much I struggled to comprehend about the adults in my life. Only a sibling, I felt, would be able to understand and talk about these relationships with me.

BECAUSE HER FIRST LANGUAGE WAS FRENCH, MAL ONLY read me the French versions of nursery rhymes and fairy tales. Prior to starting school, I became as proficient in French as in English. I remember my primary teacher asking our class to repeat the letters of the alphabet as she said them. I pronounced each one in French.

That first school was Miss Perrin School, a place within walking distance from home. Teachers there used star grading: Everything was marked with a star. If you did well in a certain skill, you received a gold star. If you did poorly, a blue star. I remember being about six years old the first time I didn't get a gold star for good behavior. I was so worried about this and soon learned the reason: Apparently I was quite bossy playing hopscotch.

From Miss Perrin's, I went to the private and much larger Allen Stevenson School at 78th and Lexington. It was an all-boys school, and I liked it very much. But almost as soon as I began there, I started getting terrible sinus pains. My head would feel awfully heavy for long periods, and I would sometimes miss up to three days a week because of illness. The worst attacks came at inopportune times—I missed one of my own birthday parties because I felt so badly.

It soon became more normal for me to feel ill rather than healthy. Mother kept me home from school quite often. Not because I felt sick so much as she was worried I might be contagious. When I would finally return, I was about ten miles behind all the other kids. It was very hard to catch up.

The school finally said that if my absences continued, I would need to repeat a grade. I don't think Mother took me to see a doctor until the school intervened. When she did, the doctor said I had bad sinusitis. He recommended that I go to school out West, where a drier climate would help my condition.

Through her social circle, Mother met a woman whose son had suffered from terrible asthma attacks. His condition had greatly improved, the woman said, after he spent time at a place called Arizona Desert School in Tucson. That became the plan for me.

By then my father, Hampton Robb, had married his third wife. Along with other adults, he expressed some concern about my going west as I had only ever lived in New York City. I suppose he feared what might happen to a boy like me, living more or less on his own in a place far away. I wasn't afraid. I just wanted to get rid of the god-awful sinus problem.

By the time I headed to Tucson, Mother also had remarried for the third time. My new stepfather was Army S.Sgt. Warren Patrick Barkley. Mother and "Alvin" married secretly in a ceremony in Arlington, Virginia. I never knew Alvin well, and I never understood what Mother saw in him. Mal didn't like him either. As soon as I moved west, Mal found employment with another family. Alvin left pretty soon after that. He had married Mother for her money. He squandered a good bit of it and got even more in the divorce settlement.

❖ 3 ❖

I'll never forget arriving at the Arizona Desert School, located just outside of Tucson. Spanish-style architecture dotted the school's campus. Eager to see which building held my room after such a long trip, I had to wait. Staff members took new arrivals to the stables first. Before students could meet their teachers or their roommates, they met their horses.

Staff assigned a horse to each boy. During the entirety of a student's time in Tucson, he would have responsibility for this horse, which he needed to name, feed, brush, bathe, and exercise. The first lesson in caring for these animals began before we unpacked. My horse looked as if he had a butch haircut. His mane was oddly shaped, and he reminded me of a toothbrush. So that's what I named him: Toothbrush.

At 6 a.m. the next day, I awoke and went directly to the stables. Nothing could have been better for me. Someone had always been dressing and telling me what to do. Now I had an animal relying on me. I was finally in charge of something. During my three years at Arizona Desert School, I spent every free moment with Toothbrush. Students received grades for taking care of their animals, and stable hands were always around to monitor our interactions. But I didn't need a grade to motivate me. I formed an immediate bond with Toothbrush. He was the best friend I had at that time.

Arizona Desert School was small. The student population consisted of four grades of boys with about ten boys per class. Every day, we followed the same schedule. In the morning, we'd have our studies. Then in the afternoon, we would take long horseback rides in the canyons. I had learned how to ride at my uncle's farm in Connecticut, so I wasn't new to horseback riding like some of the boys. I became such a good rider that in my final year with Toothbrush, I could ride bareback and guide him with just my knees. Not everyone liked the long canyon rides, but I sure did. I loved the shape of the cactus and never tired of seeing one. We also would come across all kinds of creatures. When our leader would shoot a rattlesnake, we boys would take turns holding its carcass as we rode along. After dinner, we would maybe watch a movie and play a game outside, like Cowboys and Indians.

Nearly fifty years after "orphan trains" sent poor children from New York City streets to farms in the West, desert schooling became a popular topic of conversation among wealthy families on both coasts. Ranch schools branded themselves as rustic yet upscale locations that used an outdoors-based education to improve students' health. The ranch school (and its holiday counterpart, the dude ranch) perpetuated the same Western romantic myth as did the Hollywood western. Half of the boys enrolled came from New York City, where the school had a recruitment office.

Program directors steeped us in the history of the West. Lecturers would come with stories to accompany frontier films, and we went on lots of field trips to learn about the region. The dry air was indeed medicinal. After being sick for over a year and missing days and days of school back in New York, I was ill only one time in Arizona. That was when my father visited and took me away for a weekend to San Diego. I became so sick that, back in Tucson, they put me in the hospital. But I never had another sinus attack after that.

Tuition was, of course, quite expensive, and all of the boys were from wealthy families. I was no different. While I went to school with the sons of movie stars and politicians, they went to school with me, the great-grandson of Thomas Fortune Ryan and the grandson of Allan Ryan.

⁖ 4 ⁖

Thomas Fortune Ryan was my mother Miriam's grandfather. Born in Virginia in 1851 to Irish immigrants, by the mid-1920s, Ryan had become the tenth richest man in America.

My great-grandfather got his start in business with the help of his first employer, John Smith Barry, the owner of a Baltimore dry goods store. After hiring young Ryan, Barry soon realized that the new clerk had fallen in love with his daughter, Ida. He challenged his future son-in-law to prove that he could support a family. When he learned of his interest in business and his desire to go to New York City, he sponsored Ryan for a seat on the New York City Stock Exchange. By the turn of the century, Thomas Fortune Ryan had worked his way from brokerage clerk to partner of the famous financier William C. Whitney. Together the two formed a monopoly on municipal transportation services, starting with their consolidation of horsecar businesses.

When Whitney died in 1904, he and Ryan had amassed what *The New Yorker* later called "two of the quickest and largest fortunes in the whole era of frenzied finance." A few years later, when a jury overturned a lawsuit against Whitney's estate, it said that the business practices of Whitney and Ryan were "dishonest and probably criminal" but not "actionable."

At that time, Thomas Fortune Ryan's wealth was estimated at $50 million. He and Ida Barry Ryan lived in a mansion on Fifth Avenue that held a private chapel and an art gallery. Their collection contained three busts of Ryan sculpted by Auguste Rodin.

The press often recognized Thomas Fortune Ryan as a leading benefactor of the Democratic Party (he was a good friend to Grover Cleveland) and of the Catholic church. His money, they knew, came not only from transit but also from banking, insurance, oil, gas, coal, electricity, and tobacco. And those were only his North American interests. Ryan also had money coming from Africa, particularly the Belgian Congo and Portuguese Angola. King Leopold II partnered with Ryan in a business that held mining and mineral rights to over seven million acres. The two reaped millions from diamonds, gold, copper, lead, and lumber.

Although they filed frequent stories on Thomas Fortune Ryan's business interests and dealings, reporters were hard-pressed to get an interview from the man himself. One described Ryan as "suave and noiseless." And while they assumed my great-grandfather was religious because of the millions he gave to the church, the contributions came at the bidding of Ida Barry, a devout Catholic. Perhaps he donated so much because he felt like he owed her—Ryan had multiple affairs throughout their forty-four years of marriage. He even remarried twelve days after Ida's death in October 1917.

My grandfather Allan was the oldest of the five sons that Thomas and Ida had together. Shocked that his father planned to remarry so soon after his mother's death, Allan asked him to wait. The two had, at one point, a good enough relationship for Thomas Fortune Ryan to give his eldest son his seat on the Stock Exchange. But when he heard Allan's request to delay his marriage, Ryan disowned him. Upon the tycoon's death twelve years later, only three of his adult sons had outlived him. Two received trusts valued at over $30 million each. Allan received pearl studs valued at $14,150.

In the decade or so between the deaths of his two parents, Allan Ryan suffered a very public professional humiliation. He was as chatty with the press as his father was quiet, a trait that endeared him to reporters obsessed with stories about the Ryans. In addition to being a loyal son to his mother, Allan had a strong business acumen and killer instincts. By age twenty-eight, he was close personally and profession-ally with Charles Schwab. Two years after his mother died, during the bull market year of 1919, one reporter wrote that Allan Ryan was the "mightiest bull of them all."

Recognizable by his large mustache and sad-looking eyes, Allan Ryan also was a sickly man. He and his wife, whom I knew as "Granny Ryan," raised six children in their Murray Hill home. One room there often served as a sick ward for my grandfather. In 1920, seemingly at the top of his professional game, he made a very poor calculation while recovering from an illness. On a visit to the house, a colleague expressed concern that shareholders were plotting to force Allan Ryan out of his shares in Stutz Motors, one of my grandfather's strongest investments. Stutz at the time was having ups and downs, but it was riding high on its Bearcat. I can best describe the Bearcat as a midlife-crisis sports car.

In 1920, the New York Stock Exchange was growing in power and did not yet have any type of public regulation. Members governed themselves, with the wealthiest and most powerful changing rules on whims that benefited their investments and punished those of their competitors. When Allan Ryan believed that shareholders were trying to force him out, he used this gap in regulation to figure out how to buy *them* out. And he almost did. Borrowing a million dollars from Charles Schwab and millions more from banks, he manipulated and bought enough shares to form a corner in the market.

His plan backfired when the shareholders allied against him. Facing bankruptcy, Allan went to his father. He hoped that Thomas Fortune would look past his comment, made in the grief of losing his mother. Allan asked his dad to help him as surely—and only—he could. Thomas Fortune Ryan refused. Allan was kicked out of the New York Stock Exchange and fell into bankruptcy. Overall, the Bearcat event had cost over $32 million.

When my great grandfather died in 1928, *The New York Times* wrote that Thomas Fortune Ryan was the "sole survivor of a group of rich New York men whose power and personalities were known and felt throughout the US and who posed for the first composite picture of 'Big Business.'"

Even though he had refused a trust for his son Allan, my great grandfather did remember his nine grandchildren, including Allan's six children. Each, including my mother, received between $3 million and $6 million. Allan's two brothers squandered their trusts. Their fortunes made them irresponsible, and even with millions in the bank, they allowed accounts to fall delinquent. At one point, Saks Fifth Avenue nailed a bill to the family's Fifth Avenue house.

⁙ 5 ⁙

Arizona Desert School dismissed its students for summer holidays but not Christmas. Mother thought I would be angry with this, but I wasn't at all. She couldn't understand why I wouldn't want to come home for Christmas dinner and open my presents under a tree.

Mother—Miriam—was the second of six children born to Allan and Sarah Ryan. She had four brothers and one sister: Allan Jr., Ted, Peter, Barry, and Sally. My four uncles played a big role in my life during my childhood. They and Mother were quite close, I think because they were part of the family that had been cut off by Thomas Fortune. The brothers loved her and she loved them.

The three older boys had served in World War II before finding success in business or politics. Allan Jr. operated a molded latex and mining business, and served as the director of the Belgian American Banking Corporation. He and brother Peter also ran the Royal Typewriter Company, considered the family's main business.

Ted (my namesake) was a spy in the Office of Strategic Services and a great skier. A Yale graduate, he became a Connecticut state senator for multiple terms. When his father died, Ted inherited a Connecticut farm that became a gathering spot for our family. Ted and Allan Ryan bonded over their love of showing their herds of Black Angus cattle at breeding competitions. Peter and Barry were breeders and owners of thoroughbred racehorses.

I spent a good amount of time with Peter Ryan and his wife, Anne. Of their four children, their daughter Suzannah was exactly my age, and we got along fabulously. She was the closest thing I had to a sibling. We both loved to dance and went to countless dances together. I would often play games where I would start dancing with Suzannah and then trade partners, leaving her to fend for herself as I danced with a young lady who really interested me. Boy, could I anger Suzannah! Once on a summer vacation in Canada, Suzannah got so mad at me during a tennis match that she broke her racquet over my head.

Peter Ryan became the president of a golf club near his vacation home in Canada. Suzannah and I had a lot of fun playing golf and tennis and running around the club grounds. She and I stayed in touch throughout our lives until she died of cancer as a young mother. When Suzannah passed, I started seeing more of her younger sister, Cynthia. Every now and then I take the train into New York City and we go to lunch.

Barry Ryan was the youngest son, the wild one. He maintained a stable on Uncle Ted's farm in Connecticut. One of my favorite summers was spent with Uncle Barry and his wife, Gwyneth. Working with them as a stable hand, I earned the nickname "Mucksack Robb." I went with Barry to run the horses in Saratoga, Belmont, and many other places. It was so much fun. I loved spending time with jockeys and being part of the stable entourage. My time with Barry and Aunt Gwyneth was precious. I found such comfort in Gwyneth's presence in particular. She was so much fun, so warm, and so nice. When she and Barry divorced, I didn't spend any more summers on the family farm, but I did think that a life raising and racing horses might be something I wanted to do.

I was blessed with great uncles and aunts. I benefited from the fact that they all liked my mother. They also shared a difficult relationship with their own mother.

Every Christmas Day in New York City, the Ryan siblings and their children would assemble at Granny Ryan's apartment. She was quite the grand dame and could be a royal pain. Nobody wanted to have much to do with her. I remember knowing that I—and everybody—had to behave. You wore your very best clothes, you didn't touch her breakables, and whatever happened, you didn't upset Granny Ryan. She made it very clear if you were disruptive. Cynthia remembers her father, Peter, taking his four children to visit Granny once a month. Propped up on satin pillows and wearing many strands of pearls, Granny would nod at the children lined up at the foot of her bed. She would point her cigarette holder, made from mother of pearl, at each child and ask for their name and grade. Then she would nod at Peter, saying "Thank you for bringing the children," and indicate it was time for them to leave.

Even though Granny could be insufferable toward their wives, Granny's sons didn't challenge her. They just went along with the drill. Everybody went to Granny gatherings with their tails between their legs trying to figure out how to quickly get them over with. When Granny became ill, my mother looked after her health. Granny was cold and judgmental—it wasn't easy to spend time in the same room with her, much less take care of her physical ills. Before I was born, my grandfather Allan had left the Murray Hill house. Divorcing Granny, he sent her and his six children to Europe for a year when he married a woman whom we all called "Aunt Irene."

We all loved Aunt Irene. Younger, friendlier, and as warm as could be, Irene was the polar opposite of Granny. I remember seeing Irene at certain events and Granny at others well past my grandfather's death in 1940. But I never quite put together why the women were never in the same room or at the same gathering.

There was one Ryan sibling who didn't seem welcome to the family reunions. Although Uncle Barry was the "wild" one, Aunt Sally, the youngest child, was the one the family treated shamefully.

Aunt Sally was an artistic talent who frowned upon her family's social climbing. Mother and Peter occasionally met with Sally, but for the life of me, I couldn't figure out why she wasn't welcome to the larger family dinners. The few times I met Sally as a child, I found her very pleasant.

Mal was the one who eventually told me—much later, when I was in college—that Sally was a lesbian. Even in my early twenties, I didn't know exactly what the word "lesbian" meant. I had to look it up in the dictionary.

Sally's career as a painter and sculptor started in her mid-twenties, when she exhibited a piece at the Royal Academy of Arts in Toronto. She later studied with sculptor Jean Camus in Paris and had work shown at the Royal Academy of Arts in London. At one point, Sally became close with the famous British sculptor Jacob Epstein and his wife, artist Kathleen Garman. The three lived as a ménage à trois for some time, and their collected work today is part of the Garman Ryan Collection at the New Art Gallery Walsall in England.

After I graduated from Yale, I went out of my way to catch up with Sally. We shared many coffee dates. Sally never spoke of her family, but I figured she had lived on Ryan money until she established herself as a successful sculptor.

From Mal, I learned that when the family realized Sally's sexual preference, some members treated her as if she suffered from a social disease they might contract.

I gained enormous respect and love for Sally. She was the first person really who exposed me to the world of arts. She took me to my first opera and helped me appreciate it. I learned so much from her, even though she died in London at age fifty-one. Lung cancer killed her, just as it had Granny Ryan by that time.

❧ 6 ❧

I didn't really know Sally until decades after my Christmases spent at Arizona Desert School. When the school
first opened in 1927, the headmaster asked parents not
to send large gifts at Christmastime. There was an obvious
economic disparity between life on the school's campus
and life in the greater Tucson area, and the school wanted
its students to value charity. Regulating Christmas presents
was one way to de-emphasize materialism.

But parents, especially those feeling guilty about sending their sons to boarding school, didn't listen. Rooms
became full of every gift that a wealthy boy might want. So
the school developed a new strategy to develop the student
social conscience. By the time I arrived, Arizona Desert
School had adopted a wonderful tradition.

Every Christmas Day, staff took us to one of two orphan-
ages—either St. Joseph's or the Arizona Children's Home—
and paired each student with a younger orphan boy who
he took back to school for the day. I remember spending
Christmas with the same boy two years in a row. I valued
that time more than any upper-crust New York holiday party.

We spent most of the day on our school campus, entertaining and encouraging the younger boys. After a turkey
dinner together, we would play games. Some years we
exchanged gifts. We students would give the orphans things
like baseball gloves, and the younger boys would give us
something they made in a workshop. I remember how much

they loved riding the horses and having someone dote on them for an entire day. Never before these Christmases had it dawned on me that there was even such a thing as an orphan. The school taught me for the first time to appreciate that there were people my age who were much poorer than I was.

BOYS OUR AGE FROM THE GREATER TUCSON AREA OCCA-sionally would come on campus. Once a year, sometime around Christmas, the school sponsored an annual rodeo that hundreds of locals would attend. We students would compete in Pony Express races, polo, and horse jumping competitions. There was something called pig sticking, where riders would throw spears into pigs, and quadrille, a type of musical chairs that you would play on horseback.

Polo was my favorite event. Because I was such a good horseback rider, I played quite well. The school had a polo team, and in my last year, when I was in seventh grade, we won the state's junior high championship. That was a real highlight.

By then, one thing about Arizona Desert School had begun to worry me. I knew that the academics weren't very strong. Without much effort, I was first or second in my class of ten. I had no study habits, and I had never failed a test. I remember once thinking to myself, "Is this all there is?"

Clearly, the school was there to nurture our health over all else. I knew that when I returned east, I was heading to prep school somewhere in New England. That type of school, I sensed, would have a very different type of classroom.

Ted Robb

❧ 7 ❧

Once a week in Arizona, I would write to Mother. That was largely because the school emphasized letter writing. Mother wrote but never visited. That was okay. I knew she wouldn't enjoy it there at all.

For two or three months every summer, I would return to New York City. I couldn't wait for the day to come when I would get back on the train and head west, following the conductor around as he punched tickets. I didn't disdain New York, but life in Tucson was so different in every possible way. Going home in the summer was like having a second life. Mal was gone, but she had taught me my role very well. I could dress myself up and go through the motions. When Mother's third marriage had ended, her evening cocktail parties increased. I was still young enough to parade around the living room. Only now, without Mal, I would disappear into the evening by going back to my room alone.

During the day, however, with nobody else in the apartment, Mother and I spent more time together than ever before. We started talking a little bit more about things. Occasionally Jimmy came up.

JIMMY HEBERT WAS MY HALF-BROTHER AND MOTHER'S only other child. Four years older than me, Jimmy would visit Mother (and stay in my room) for one month every summer. Jimmy had a physical handicap connected to a birth defect. He blamed Mother fiercely for it. She had only lived with him when he was a baby; within a year of his birth, she had divorced her first husband, Jimmy's father, and married Hampton Robb, my father.

Mother's first husband was a man named Jacques Hebert, a Canadian aviator and politician. Granny Ryan had met Hebert while on a trip to Montreal. Noticing that he was quite the eligible bachelor, she summoned Mother from New York City. Mother lived in Montreal for a while, long enough to surprise her friends when they opened a copy of *Quest* magazine and read that she had eloped.

Mother's brothers never took to Jacques Hebert. They could tell he didn't treat her well. When she left him for my father, Hebert kept full custody of Jimmy and raised him in Montreal. Jimmy grew up hearing his father talk about the reason for his birth defect: Jacques Hebert told him, again and again, that Mother drank while she was pregnant. Jimmy firmly believed that his handicap was her fault. Every summer, Jimmy would visit Mother in New York and find ways to upset her. For a full month every year, he would accuse her of ruining his life. He resented her. I resented that he stayed in my room.

I don't remember these visits occurring after I went to Arizona, because I remember Mal's presence during Jimmy's visits. Mal knew, as did Mother and I, that Jimmy had an agenda for every second of every visit. He could make Mother very upset in a heartbeat. Mal had a type of relationship with Jimmy because he knew French, and they both liked speaking it to each other. But when he would start a fight with Mother, Mal didn't intervene. She would take me from the scene.

I couldn't believe the things that Jimmy told me his father said about how nasty and terrible Mother was.

Jimmy scared me. He was a bully and envious of my place in Mother's house.

Eventually, Jimmy Hebert sued Mother for negligence. Their lawyers reached a settlement. Jimmy had a hard time holding down a job, and for many years, Mother's fourth (and last) husband worried that he would come around demanding more money.

Fortunately, Jimmy's disposition changed for the better when he married. At some point, he met an older woman named Elizabeth who worked for the Canadian postal service. I liked her very much. She had a wonderful way of keeping him in check when he became irrational. Both Jimmy and his wife came to know my wife and kids, and she, in particular, loved my family. He predeceased her, and when she died, I learned that she bequeathed a generous amount of money to two of my grandchildren.

Jimmy and I never found common ground as adults. When we occasionally met, we didn't speak much. Too much damage had occurred when we were boys. To my best knowledge, he and Mother never reached a peace either.

: 8 :

A rizona was so recuperative for me. It was sad when my time there came to an end, particularly because I had to leave Toothbrush. I asked Mother if we could somehow bring the horse east, but I suppose that wasn't possible. Saying good-bye to my horse was heartbreaking. Some boys had reluctantly taken care of their horses. They saw the relationship as a duty that they resented. To my knowledge, I was the only boy in my class who became so connected to his horse.

I knew it was time to leave Arizona Desert School. My sinus trouble had all but disappeared, and my health was very good. Although I wouldn't have traded my time there for anything, I would pay a large academic price for my recuperation.

MOTHER WAS NOT HAPPY WITH MY ATTITUDE WHEN I came back. By now, I was on the brink of my teenage years. We went on a European vacation together that summer after my seventh-grade year. Boy, was I a pill. On tours through Europe's finest museums, I sure let her know how boring the whole trip felt.

I also didn't want to go on outings with our extended family, something that I had done with joy as a younger boy. Arizona had, more or less, cut me off from those Ryan family associations for a time. Mother also knew that I wasn't happy with all of the men she dated.

I knew kids like me whose parents had divorced. Each one had chosen sides. I never did. For the longest time, I harbored a hope that Mother and Dad would get back together. Sometime during my years in Arizona, I had realized that my parents still loved each other very much. When other boys would talk about their divorced parents with hostility, repeating the horrible things each said about the other, I realized that Mother and Dad never spoke badly about each other. Both had a gentle tone when the other came up in conversation, and both asked—with genuine interest—how the other was doing whenever I occasionally transitioned between homes.

MIRIAM RYAN HEBERT MET HAMPTON ROBB AT A SOCIAL event in Washington, DC. Mother was there with Jacques on one of his ambassador duties, and Father was there with his first wife, the daughter of an American naval commander. Mother's son, Jimmy, was then a baby. Dad had two daughters, Roberta and Elizabeth, who were little girls at the time. Soon after meeting, Mother and Dad asked their spouses for a divorce and married each other. Three years later, I was born, and one year after that, they divorced.

Once again, the Ryan brothers were not surprised.

Dad's resume was more impressive than Jacques Hebert's. A sales manager for the National Biscuit Company (Nabisco), he also had served as an aide to Franklin Delano Roosevelt, functioning as a domestic acquisitions director. FDR also had given him an appointment as the American ambassador to Paraguay (I don't think Dad spoke a word of Spanish).

The Ryans weren't impressed. They were well aware of the fact that Dad was not as wealthy as they. And, based upon his departure from his first wife and two little girls, he didn't seem to have a good track record with women. Once again, they felt that Mother could have done better. They didn't have to work hard for Dad to understand how they felt. Hampton Robb was successful, charming, handsome, and close to FDR (Mother and Dad once shared a private breakfast with the president), but he would always be a second-class citizen to the Ryan brothers. Not to their sister, Miriam, though. Mother loved Dad in spite of his bank account, and she loved him long after they divorced.

I asked her during one of those summer afternoons home from Arizona why they weren't still married. I had known that soon after the divorce, Dad had married a woman named Gertrude Brown ("Gertie") from Colorado. I knew he didn't love her the way he loved Mother. I also had realized, after those same conversations with other boys of divorced parents, that my parents never argued about money. Dad didn't pay any child support and Mother didn't begrudge him that. She didn't ask for it or hold it over him. She had money, and he didn't. I saw this gracious attitude as further evidence of her love for Dad.

Mother didn't deny anything that I said. She had divorced my father, she told me, because he had been caught with another woman. Mother made it clear to me that she believed people "don't get seconds on something like that."

Later I would learn that my father's mistress had been my stepmother, Gertie. I don't know the exact sequence of events, but before Mal's arrival, Mother and I moved to West Palm Beach, Florida, for a time. It was there that she filed for divorce, citing "mental cruelty," a charge she never mentioned to me. The papers said Hampton had been trying to separate her from her brothers' influence.

Reporters wrote that Dad had been keeping Mom from paying child support to Jimmy. This part makes sense to me, as I knew that Jacques had sued Mother for $25,000 in child support expenses.

Mother never spoke of these things to me. All I knew for most of my life was that Dad's affair with Gertie ended their marriage.

⁘ 9 ⁘

About a year after I came back from Tucson, I visited Dad and Gertie at their home in New Canaan, Connecticut. Gertie drank quite a bit. When she drank, she turned into a sloppy mess. As much as I loved Dad, I hated being with her, especially because I could see her pushing booze onto him.

On this particular stay, I was alone with Gertie at the house one afternoon when I realized that she had been in the bathroom for quite some time. She had started drinking at noon that day, and as her behavior only got worse with every drink, I had tried to avoid her. But I could sense something was wrong.

Knocking on the bathroom door, I soon tried the handle and realized she had locked herself inside. I called the police before calling Dad. When the officers arrived, they broke down the door and pulled an unconscious Gertie from the tub. At some point, I remember Dad sitting me down and telling me that I had saved Gertie from committing suicide. I must have asked why he had married her. That was when he admitted that he had always loved my mother and had made a mistake.

I realize now that my stepmother's near suicide could have traumatized me. I think it didn't so much because I knew Gertie was an alcoholic and very unstable. By then I also was overwhelmed with my studies at Pomfret.

Ted Robb

The academic demands on my time kept me thinking of nothing more than keeping up with my classmates. Most of my Tucson peers had needed to repeat a grade when they returned home from Arizona Desert School. I was one of only two from my class there who had stayed on track.

⁙ 10 ⁙

D ad had chosen Pomfret for me. The choice marked the first time he had become involved in any large decision regarding my life. Nobody on either side of the family had gone to Pomfret. The Ryan brothers had attended a Catholic preparatory school called Canterbury, founded by a group of Catholic laymen that included their father, Allan. Dad had attended a private high school in Cleveland. He liked Pomfret because it started a year earlier than other preparatory schools. I began in the eighth grade, the fall after I returned home from Arizona Desert School. Pomfret also was smaller than the prestigious schools Mother had thought about, such as Andover and Exeter. Dad was very sensitive to this issue of class size. He knew I would do better with smaller numbers. I was one of ten in all of my Arizona classes, and most Eastern prep schools held between twenty-five and thirty students per class.

Mother wasn't thrilled at first with the idea of Pomfret, but she spent some time reading about it and saw that it had a good history. She liked that it was the chosen school for generations of Dupont men, and she also learned that a very good friend of hers had a son who was heading there: Gil Chapman. Gil and I not only attended Pomfret together for five years but also went to Yale, where we were chosen for the same senior society. To this day, he is a very good friend.

POMFRET IS LOCATED IN NORTHEASTERN CONNECTICUT, near Putnam. I visited it for the first time when Dad accompanied me to my admissions interview. The headmaster was a good man named Dexter Strong. After our talk, Strong looked at me and asked, "Do you have any ideas of where you want to go to college?"

"Harvard," Dad said. It was his alma mater.

Out of the blue, for reasons I still don't understand, I blurted "Williams."

Dexter Strong smiled. He had gone to Williams. I had no idea.

Dad got a good laugh out of that. He said I would make a good politician one day.

IN SO MANY WAYS, POMFRET WAS THE BEST POSSIBLE place for me. Eighth graders lived together in the lower dormitory, out of the spotlight and away from the older boys. We bonded quickly. Dad was right—Pomfret's small class sizes were very manageable, and its tight-knit community attracted students from other prep schools, where large classes and difficult academics alienated certain types of students. I certainly may have drowned in a more competitive, less personal environment.

I had sensed at Arizona Desert School that I had fallen very far behind my peers back east. Once Pomfret began, I realized immediately that I was correct. Without study skills, I was hard-pressed to complete all of my assignments. Most courses were very challenging for me. Latin, in particular, was hard, probably because the teacher was so fierce. But even in English, where I had a wonderful teacher, the homework was difficult.

Every night I had to write a report for English class. The teacher let us students pick the topic and write whatever we wanted, but that freedom of choice made the open-ended assignment harder for me. I just remember feeling so down as I tackled that homework. I knew that the next day, the teacher would read aloud what we had written. Then we students would discuss one another's ideas, provide verbal or written feedback, and sometimes write response essays. We wrote constantly. It was torture. But that class was exactly what I needed. It gave me a wake-up call. Those nightly English assignments forced me to develop study hours and habits. When I graduated from Pomfret, I made a special effort to go back and thank that teacher—his name was Bob Dentler—for putting me to the test. Dentler could remember just how hard that first year had been for me.

As I entered ninth grade, I felt more relaxed. I had developed a little more confidence academically and knew that I could find a way to handle the work. And I did, in spite of playing three sports a year (football, basketball, and baseball) for the next four years. I think Coach Mansfield was a big reason why I loved spending so much time on the ball fields.

Baseball was my best sport. I played catcher, and my senior year, I was the team captain. Coach and I became quite close, largely because we spent more time together than ever before. Literally. One of our games that year was the longest played in the school's history up to that time.

Coach Mansfield became a father figure and taught me a lot about nutrition and mental toughness. My teammates and I knew that whatever advice he gave us would be good and that we could apply it to life beyond the court or field. He encouraged me to go beyond whatever I thought I might be able to do.

One piece of advice stands out. When we felt like we would be outmatched in a game, Coach would repeat the same line to keep our heads level.

"They get in their pants just like you do—one leg at a time."

I still think about that. Sometimes the simplest image is the best.

·11·

Mother and Dad would both visit, but never at the same time. Mother liked watching me play every sport but football. She hated the tackling. The first time she visited for a game, someone on the other team absolutely flattened me on the field. Mother was so worried, and so incensed, that she started charging the field until someone held her back. The other boys later laughed about that.

By then, Mother and I had developed more of a relationship. I think that traveling together helped with this. One place we visited often was Bermuda. The first time she took me, I had just had my wisdom teeth removed, and she hoped the scenery would cheer me up. Later, I fell head over heels for a beautiful young lady I met at Coral Beach.

We also had taken that European vacation together the summer before Pomfret started. What I remember most from that trip was my utter rejection of the museums that I toured with Mother. Constantly complaining of boredom, I realized then that I had the ability to make people miserable with my temperament. There was one sight that I appreciated though: After meeting a group of southern schoolgirls on the ship, we ran into them a few times on our European trek. There were about ten of them, and they were the most gorgeous young ladies I had ever seen.

About two or three years later, I returned to Europe with a Pomfret friend. He and I followed a similar itinerary.

I remember that he was in love with a girl back home, and this time, he was the miserable one. Constantly moaning, he clearly wanted to be with the girl more than with me. Halfway through the trip, I said, "Why don't you just go home then?"

He did (and he eventually married that girl). I stayed in Europe by myself and visited the same museums that I had hated touring with Mother. This time, the Louvre, the Prado, and so many others just enchanted me. At some point, I sat down and wrote Mother a long letter apologizing for the grief I had given her. I told her how much I loved being in Europe, and how I had gained some understanding of all I had closed my eyes to before. She showed me the letter when I got home. I was surprised at how much it had meant to her.

⸱ 12 ⸱

Bob Ellinger was in our lives at that time. Mother had married him, her fourth husband, during my sophomore year at Pomfret. They would stay married until her death thirty years later. A short time after the wedding ceremony, I learned that the two had met through Dad! He and Bob Ellinger had been friends and business associates, and Mother had known Bob for years.

"What a strange turn of events," I remember thinking.

Neither man ever spoke much to me about the other. I know that they had a mutual respect. Bob and I would have our ups and downs, but I could tell that he was good for Mother. He took care of her. She had started drinking more, and he had a way of curbing that habit. It was a relief, really, that he was there.

Bob Ellinger owned franchises of the Mayflower Coffee Shop. I still remember their jingle: "As you wander on through life, whatever be your goal, keep your eye upon the donut, and not upon the hole."

Once a month, Bob would send a box of doughnuts to me at my Pomfret dormitory. The other boys would rush to get one. They were a hit with all but Coach Mansfield, who warned me about overeating. I was really round as a young man, and Mansfield would say Bob's doughnuts weren't helping. He even gave me the nickname "Donuts."

Through his business connections, Bob Ellinger knew the families of two of my Pomfret roommates: Ed Dupont and Roger Bensinger. Both of these guys were hilarious.

Ed was my freshman roommate, and together we served as "dorm assistants." It was our job to keep everyone in line according to Pomfret's dormitory rules. Every night, we'd walk the corridors and make sure everyone was behaving in their rooms. We loved to tease our charges. I used to jump on Ed's back, and he would quietly walk through the halls, then jump into a room, where we'd shock the kids and start some kind of ruckus. There really weren't many discipline problems at Pomfret. Sometimes I'd catch kids smoking cigarettes. You bet I turned them in! They would get mad at me, but I saw it as my responsibility. Plus, I didn't like people smoking.

Roger Bensinger was the kind of classmate who always skated on the thinnest ice. He just loved to test authority, and I, someone who was quite obedient, was enamored by his gall. During our senior year, he joined me on a panty raid with about a half-dozen other guys. One of our classmates, Chuck Henry, had a sister who attended the storied Miss Porter's School for Girls, one of our sister schools. He got her to assemble some of her friends at a dormitory window one evening, and around dinner time, we snuck onto Miss Porter's campus and gathered below the dorm.

"Throw us your panties!" we called.

As knickers came showering down, other girls not involved alerted the dorm parents, and soon the headmaster found out. We had planned for this possibility. Two exchange students had come with us—one guy from Australia and another mischievous fellow from Spain named Carlos Androtti. These two had volunteered to step forward as the responsible parties if we got caught. When security started following us, we leaped into the car and circled the campus, leaving the foreign students behind. They gave their home addresses in Australia and Spain, confusing the guards.

Eventually, the headmistress figured it out and called Pomfret. There wasn't really anything they could do. We had trespassed, perhaps, but nobody had gotten hurt.

We kept the panties.

⁕ 13 ⁕

Among Pomfret's social highlights were quarterly dances with our sister schools. I loved nothing more than dancing. Mother deserves the credit for this. She had sent me to dancing school as a child, and as a result, I always had confidence on the dance floor.

I still remember my first social dance. It was before I moved to Arizona, so I couldn't have been older than eight. I remember the teacher lining the girls on one side of the room and the boys on the other. She was very proper, and I can still hear her voice.

"It's very important how you make an introduction to the lady you are going to dance with."

The first time she told the boys to choose a partner, there was a mad rush from one side of the room toward the other. I thought that was a little nuts, so I slowly strolled behind the others. The teacher clapped her hands and demanded our attention. She sent all the boys back to their side.

"There was only one young man who listened," she said. "Ted, you go over and select a dance partner first." Oh, did I turn sixteen colors of the rainbow. But I picked somebody immediately.

Ten years or so later, I went to all of the dances shared by Pomfret and the Ethel Walker School for Girls. I still have a couple of my old dance cards. It was up to the man, before the dance, to walk around and ask girls to dance with him. The girls would write their names on our cards, and that way we had an itinerary for the evening and there was less awkward-ness between dances. I often cheated though. We were only supposed to have no more than one dance with any one girl, but I would find someone I liked and have her sign multiple lines. Someone named Jane appears quite a bit on one card.

In addition to dances and sports, Pomfret's social activi-ties included acting, choral and instrumental groups, a school newspaper, a history club, and multiple art classes. The campus also had a golf course where I spent many hours.

We students would look the same in our tie and blaz-ers sporting the school's insignia and motto. *Certa Veriliter* means "Strive Valiantly," but we would joke that it really meant "Certainly Virile." The school, though, instilled in us a brotherhood that went beyond the uniform.

Through service and social activities, Pomfret made an effort to emphasize the importance of each individual within the student body. For example, nobody was too wealthy or popular to avoid waiting on tables in the dining hall. This was a job that every student took a turn in shar-ing. I happened to love it, especially when I could serve as head waiter and order people around.

From the moment a student stepped on campus, he became a member of one of two teams: the Ionians or the Achaeans. He would remain on that team until the day he graduated. This way, whenever the school had pick-up games or a competition of a different sort, each boy knew where he stood. Nobody would be left last in line nor passed over by captains selecting teams. The competition climaxed in an annual tug-of-war match that involved the entire student body. Whichever team won earned bragging rights for the year. This type of team structure kept athletes from dominating the social hierarchy.

But as much as I felt a part of this Pomfret brand, I began to recognize how privileged I was attending a private school. This realization made me yearn for something that I couldn't yet articulate: something that would drive a very important decision in my college years and set me on a course that many in my family would never understand.

⁚14⁚

ometimes I tell myself that I was groomed to be a very narrow-minded person. One reason why I say this is because I didn't go to school with any Black or Jewish students at Arizona Desert School or Pomfret. There was also very little economic disparity among students. At Pomfret, a few "poorer" students lived locally and attended as day students. I don't remember anybody antagonizing them because they didn't have as much money. If anything, they were sought after as experts on stores and fun places to go in the area. But most of the people I attended school with—at Miss Perrin's, at Allan Stevenson, at Arizona Desert School, at Pomfret, and even at Yale—looked the same.

If pressed, I could say that I was a minority at Pomfret. I was one of three students who identified as Roman Catholic. Ironically, in Pomfret and in Arizona, this religious affiliation put me in closer proximity to people of color than anyone else experienced on campus. It often was left to "the help" to escort me back and forth from campus to Mass. More people in the kitchen shared my religious faith than did my classmates. I didn't think this through at the time. I never once thought to strike up any kind of association with those who took me to church.

I went to Mass every single week while at boarding school. This attendance was due more to my being a creature of habit than a fervent religious follower. Pomfret was a school that followed a very high Episcopalian liturgy in chapel on weekdays and Sunday mornings. Even as a Catholic student, I was required to attend these services. I didn't mind though. I would go to Mass early in town at 8 a.m. and then join my classmates in chapel at 10 a.m. I learned to appreciate Protestant services. Catholic churches didn't sing hymns at the time, and Protestant ones did. It made those services more palatable.

The Robb side of the family was Episcopalian, but Dad didn't go to church. The Ryans weren't particularly religious either, even though they were raised Catholic and had attended private religious schools. Mother's grandparents, Thomas Fortune and Ida Barry Ryan, had contributed millions to St. Jean Baptiste and other Catholic buildings, but Mother didn't really attend services. Because of her three divorces, the church denied Mother's participation in ecclesiastical activities like Communion. Among the adults in my life, it was Mal who had instilled in me a connection to Catholicism.

At Pomfret, where I was one of three Catholics, I began to understand that religion was a private thing for me. I saw it as something that I needed as I grew older. As I became more aware of existential questions, I felt a peace knowing that the church had answers. I didn't know what those answers were, but I knew that they existed somewhere, and that comforted me. I didn't feel uncomfortable being in the religious minority at Pomfret.

For a time, I would at Yale.

⁖ 15 ⁖

Growing up, I always thought I'd attend Harvard. So did Dad.

Dad had grown up in the Midwest and came east to attend Harvard. So had his brother Philip, younger by six years. I don't know much more about their adolescence than that. Much of their early lives is a mystery to me.

I never met my grandfather Hunter Robb, a renowned gynecologist who raised his sons in Cleveland. Originally from Burlington, New Jersey, Hunter Robb graduated from the University of Pennsylvania in 1884. Over the next ten years, he served at the Kensington Hospital for Women in Philadelphia, remaining in practice there even after he moved to Baltimore to become chair of Gynecology and Obstetrics at Johns Hopkins University. There he met my grandmother.

Born and raised in Ontario, Canada, Isabel Adams Hampton ("Addie") worked as a rural schoolteacher after graduating from high school. Frustrated with her limited professional choices, she left for New York City at age twenty to study nursing. There wasn't much for her to study. Isabel became frustrated with her courses at the Bellevue Training School for Nurses. She couldn't believe there was so little to read about the profession and such a poorly organized curriculum. After moving to Chicago to start her career as a registered nurse, she began writing her own programs and texts. Isabel organized the American Nurses Association and served as its first president. Her leadership efforts were noticed. She became the first superintendent of nurses at Johns Hopkins University Hospital, selected from a field of one-hundred applicants.

Soon after Hunter Robb met the brilliant, tall, and blue-eyed Isabel Hampton, he proposed marriage. The engagement surprised the medical community, which correctly assumed that Isabel, a well-known nurse and author, would leave her position to focus on having a family. She and Hunter wed in 1894, the same year that both published their first books: Isabel penned *Nursing: Its Principles and Practice*, and Hunter wrote *Aseptic Surgical Technique*, a pioneering text for surgeons in limiting patient shock.

When the two married in London, Isabel carried a bridal bouquet sent from her friend Florence Nightingale. After a honeymoon spent touring Europe's leading medical research centers, the Robbs moved to Cleveland, Ohio. There, Hunter chaired the Gynecology Department at Lakeside Hospital. Isabel didn't practice as a nurse again, but she did teach in the nurse's training school at Lakeside, Ohio. Maintaining her professional associations and memberships, she wrote two more books: *Nursing Ethics: For Hospital and Private Use* and *Educational Standards for Nurses*. From what I understand, her work focused on teaching not only the principles of chemistry, anatomy, physiology, and other sciences but also how to practically apply this knowledge.

I didn't know anything about my grandmother's career until my children were grown. When Dad was fifteen, a streetcar hit his mother and instantly killed her. She was on her way to pick Dad up from a dance class, and I've always wondered whether Dad felt some level of guilt and that's why he never spoke about her or his childhood.

After Isabelle's death, Hunter Robb was engaged to the mother of one of Hampton's college roommates; some time after that ended, my grandfather married a New York nurse named Marion Wilson in 1929. The marriage lasted for about a decade before my grandfather died of pneumonia. Jealous of Isabel Hampton Robb's professional accomplishments, Marion destroyed many of my grandmother's papers and belongings.

About twenty years ago, I received a phone call from a friend who had recently had surgery at Johns Hopkins University Hospital. While walking the hallways in recovery, she had come across a portrait of a beautiful woman. Her name, she saw on the placard, was Isabel Hampton Robb. She wondered if we were related. That phone call set me on a research quest to learn what I could about my grandmother. I've since had the opportunity to support a fund at the Johns Hopkins University School for Nurses that had been started in her name.

Of all of the storied figures on either side of my family, Isabel Adams Hampton Robb is the one I wish I could have met. I would have loved the chance to talk with her.

⁂ 16 ⁂

E ven though I didn't know Hunter or Isabelle, my pater-
nal grandparents, I came to love a place that meant a
great deal to them both: Cap-à-l'Aigle, Canada.

Every summer I spent two weeks there with Dad, who
had learned from his father to rent lakes from the Canadian
government as vacation destinations during the summer
season. This measure allowed them to protect "their" fishing grounds from other people.

Uncle Philip, Dad's brother, had a house in Murray Bay,
a Quebecois village north of Quebec City on the shore of
the St. Lawrence River, near Cap-à-l'Aigle. Decades before,
my grandmother had built a vacation home there for nurses.
She eventually turned it over to a nurses' association that
maintained it until the home fell into disrepair. Uncle Philip
then purchased the house and turned it into a family holiday spot. Dad and I always visited Philip, his wife, Mary,
and their three daughters on our way to the fishing lakes
where the family leased property. These Canadian summer
vacations held some of the best memories of my childhood.
Philip and Mary embraced me into their family, and being
with my older cousins was so much fun.

Philip had moved his family to Canada from Long
Island during World War II. Working for the War Department, he became worried about a German invasion after
stories surfaced of enemy submarines off of New York's
coast. Among other things, it was a good business deci-

sion. Philip Robb later sold bitters, including the Angostura brand. Before becoming popular in cocktails, the bitters had a medicinal use; military doctors used them to help soothe soldiers' upset stomachs. During the Prohibition years, Uncle Philip's business blossomed: he didn't have as many competitors in Canada as he did in New York.

EVERY YEAR, I COULDN'T WAIT TO GO TO CANADA WITH Dad. The trips always had some element of mystery. I loved moving from the New York sidewalks to the Canadian outdoors, where we would fish, hunt, canoe, escape, and explore. I don't think Dad ever completely relaxed anywhere else. He was always knee-deep in his work as a salesman. Canada was our only time to be truly alone together. Gertie wasn't much of a camper so she often stayed in Connecticut.

Mal could sense she needed to have a low profile in Canada. Philip's family never took to her. They thought that Mother had taken the easy route in hiring her and that Mal was too controlling. Whenever we would arrive at the start of the vacation, Mal would have me dressed to the nines. I think Dad had asked Mother not to send her along, but she thought I needed to have her close by. I didn't ever really feel relaxed under Mal's eye in front of the Robbs. I knew she drove Uncle Philip and his three daughters nuts. They didn't like seeing me, the only Robb grandson, so micromanaged.

How I loved my beautiful cousins. Oh, I was on cloud nine when I was with those girls! I fell in love with all of them. At one point, to my disappointment, someone said, "Ted, you can't marry your cousins."

My cousin Bobbie was two years older, and she delighted in getting me to rebel against Mal. She was something. She was so happy that I put myself into her skilled hands to see what trouble we could get into together. I remember her sneaking me wine and my first cigarette. Unable to inhale, I coughed and coughed, and she laughed and laughed. Back in New York, I later had the impression that girls liked guys who smoked. Wanting to appear as a smooth operator, I would go to the drugstore around the corner and convince the owner to sell me a pack. Mother would have been livid. But she didn't have to worry. After a date told me how silly I looked, that was the end of my cigarette escapades.

LEAVING MAL IN CAP-À-L'AIGLE AT UNCLE PHILIP'S house, Dad and I would drive toward a cabin he had built on a lake. He would park the car on the side of the road, where he would leave it for days on end, and together we backpacked to the cabin. The only other person who would join us was a guide named Edgar Bouchard.

Edgar watched our property and other sites in the lake district throughout the year. A chunky French Canadian, Edgar seemed capable of taming the wild. I always felt that if you were near Edgar, nothing bad could happen to you. Every summer he just seemed to emerge from the woods. Edgar taught me how to fish and hunt and how to handle a rifle. I tried to teach him how to swim.

Edgar and Dad got along so well. We three would portage canoes between lakes on daylong fishing trips. At night, he and Dad would tell stories. Those two could really put the liquor away.

Although Edgar personified the Canadian wilderness, ironically that's what killed him. He drowned one winter. Walking across the lake either to or from our cabin, he fell through the ice. It was incredible to hear about this. Edgar knew the land and the water so well. No man can master the elements though. The ice was thinner than he had anticipated.

The Canadian weather and waters were unpredictable in the summer as well. Once Dad and I were on a rented boat in the St. Lawrence River when a terrible storm came up. We thought we were stranded. Fortunately, a big cruise ship came along and spotted us. As the crew pulled us and the boat aboard, tourists stared at us with astonishment. We felt like native woodsmen.

᛬17᛬

Dad was a great wordsmith. He could take something and make it sound ten times better than it was. That's what made him such a great salesman. I remember seeing him in professional action only one time. I don't know when Dad first became a salesman. I know that he took a leave of absence from Harvard after his junior year to join World War I over Hunter's objections. Flying had always fascinated him, so he joined the nascent Air Force and spent a year abroad as a pilot. At some point, he was shot down in Belgium. French saved him. Dad spoke it so well that the Belgians didn't turn him over to the Germans. Soon after leaving Belgium he made his way back to Harvard and finished his senior year. I remember that he kept in touch with a couple of the Belgians who rescued him.

After he graduated from Harvard, Dad became very active in the Democratic Party and helped candidates campaign. Somehow he joined Franklin Delano Roosevelt's team, and the president rewarded Dad's service with the position of Government Accounting Office (GAO) director. In this position, he purchased necessary supplies for the government. He stayed in government service for a time after marrying Mother, then transitioned into marketing and sales as the director of the National Biscuit Company.

WHEN I WAS ABOUT FIFTEEN, DAD AND I HAD SCHEDULED time together around one of his business visits to Boston. He was selling a stain remover called Renuzit and had hoped to make a pitch to the head of A&P in Boston, but the man had to cancel the daytime appointment. Dad pressed him to reschedule that very evening. The man agreed and invited us both to his house, where he hoped they could hold a quick meeting.

As soon as the front door opened, I could tell the man's wife was furious with him for bringing work home. Her husband tried to calm her down, but she was set in her frustration. She accompanied us into the living room, where Dad pulled out a pen and an inkwell and began his big pitch as if nothing were wrong at all. I squirmed and watched him maintain his cool. The atmosphere grew heavier. Dad started writing a few things down as part of his presentation, and then the inkwell in his lap fell on the woman's beautiful rug. I thought lightning was going to come out of the sky and strike us dead. She hadn't liked us to begin with, and now she was going to do God knows what. I remember worrying that she might call the police.

Dad, though, didn't miss a beat. Opening his sample case, he pulled out the stain remover.

"Now is the time to see how good this product is!" he said cheerily.

I prayed to God Almighty that the spray would work. Dad got down on his hands and knees and rubbed the carpet with the product. It disappeared. The heavy stain just vanished.

Suddenly the woman did a 180-degree turn.

"If you don't buy it, I want a carton," she said to her husband.

We stayed for dinner that night.

Later I accused Dad of purposely dropping the inkwell. He never admitted it. I would later recall his sales ability and perseverance on sales jobs of my own.

⁘ 18 ⁘

My introduction to the Ivy League was through Harvard-Yale football games. Dad would take me, and I loved standing next to him and cheering my heart out for Harvard. I could be a nasty fan, especially when Yale visited. I rooted harder for Harvard against Yale than any other team. At one such game, the Yale coach put in his captain, a senior who had just recovered from a polio scare. The player was only going on the field for an extra point play so he could get his varsity letter. The fans on both sides went wild. Then I stood up.

"Watch it!" I yelled. "It's a trick! Hit him!"

Even Dad's friends turned around and said, "Who's the ugly kid?" Dad just laughed. He was proud. Clearly, I was groomed for Harvard. Plenty of Pomfret students headed north to Harvard.

But many also went to Yale. At some point, it struck me that's where the "good guys" went, and that's where I wanted to be. Yale appeared as the all-around better choice. Plus, my cousin Nancy Ryan wanted me to go to Harvard and she really annoyed me. One day in New York City, she sat me down and told me why I had to go to Harvard. Nancy was a graduate of Radcliffe, and she insisted that Harvard was "where all the knowledge" lived. That conversation turned me off.

All of Mother's brothers had gone to Yale—even Barry (barely). Nobody pressured me to follow in their footsteps, but I did always have a connection with Uncle Ted, and I knew that he loved Yale.

So without telling Dad, I applied. I didn't apply anywhere else. And Yale waitlisted me.

I had earned superior SAT scores in my junior year but did very poorly on the test as a senior. The admissions team at Yale, I later learned, assumed I was typical of a prep school boy who goofed off during his senior year. The profile foreshadowed an academic collapse in college.

Pomfret had a reputation to maintain for placing its graduates in top collegiate programs. Because I had only applied to one school, I put that reputation in jeopardy. But instead of being frustrated with me, the Pomfret staff faulted Yale. They invited me to a faculty meeting and said they were disappointed in Yale's decision. The headmaster said that he had written the university a letter in which he threatened to dissuade future Pomfret students from applying should Yale refuse to admit me. This scared me to death. I realized Pomfret had perhaps more on the line than I did.

As I waited for Yale's decision, Pomfret helped me apply to other places. Duke and Columbia accepted me. In fact, I was in the process of filling out the paperwork to attend Columbia when I received Yale's acceptance envelope. Immediately I called Pomfret and told the headmaster. He was more than pleased.

"Now Ted, do well," he said.

I knew how far out on a limb Pomfret had gone for me. I wouldn't let them down.

POMFRET'S HEADMASTER WASN'T THE ONLY ONE TO GO out on a limb for me. When Dad had found out about the waitlisting, he was annoyed. Not because I hadn't applied to Harvard, but because Yale hadn't accepted his son.

Without my knowing, Dad contacted all of the Yale alumni he could find among his business associates. He invited them to the Harvard Club for lunch, got them liquored up, then told them a bullshit story about how I was a great quarterback and Yale would never forgive itself for passing on such a player. After spinning this yarn, he handed them all Yale stationery.

"Now write!"

Dad had each of those men pen a note on my behalf to Yale admissions citing my football prowess.

DURING MY SOPHOMORE YEAR IN NEW HAVEN, A DEAN approached me out of the blue.

"Ted, are you playing any football?" he asked.

I said I was playing intramural for Calhoun College.

"You aren't playing varsity football?" he asked.

I said I didn't think I could make the team.

He walked me to the dean's office and pulled out my file. It was much thicker than other student files. He opened it, and inside were beer-stained letters from a dozen Yale grads. Each told the director of admissions that if he didn't accept me, Yale was going to lose one of the greatest football players it could possibly get.

Later I called up Dad. "What did you do?" I asked. "You didn't tell me about this!"

He laughed. "Well, it worked, didn't it?"

When the story spread among my classmates, they gave me the nickname "Varsity Ted."

·19·

The month or two before I started at Yale, I made one of the best decisions of my life.

As Dad had anticipated, Pomfret's small class sizes were exactly the right fit for me. I had room to explore my interests, people to support me, and the opportunity to make friendships that would last a lifetime. After the initial struggle to find my academic footing, I became a gay blade. Prep school gave me wonderful, comfortable years. On visits home to New York City, I practically slept in my tuxedo as I moved from one debutante ball to the next.

But as my classmates talked more and more about college, I began to realize that I needed to create a distance from them. Regardless of whether or not Yale accepted me, I knew that I would end up somewhere with a lot of guys like myself. I either needed to make a change or enter into yet another version of high school.

I think it was Bob Dentler, the teacher who had assigned nightly eighth-grade compositions, who put in my head that Pomfret's small size was somewhat limiting. (At the time, he was planning his own entrance into bigger things. After I graduated, Dentler would earn his master's degree in sociology and become the dean of education at Columbia, then at Boston University. In 1974, he became part of a two-man team to desegregate Boston's public schools). With Dentler's words milling around in my mind, I found a way to keep myself from falling into the grips of the group that I danced my life away with at Pomfret.

Fortunately, I had the good sense to make a specific request on the roommate form that came with my Yale acceptance. Instead of choosing to room with a Pomfret man or leaving the decision to fate, I asked Yale not to place me with anyone who lived east of the Hudson River. I knew that I was eastern-oriented. My background seemed to have deputized me as a member of an Ivy League class. I wanted to be different. Admission meant a great deal to me, and I knew that I could either blow my time there and prove Yale's initial concern or surpass my expectations and meet the version of myself that Pomfret and Dad saw succeeding. The key would be a set of roommates who would challenge me.

Yale honored my request. None of my freshman roommates there had attended preparatory school, and all lived long train rides away: Peter Tomei came from Chicago, Bob Mason from Kansas City, and Rocky Suddarth from Nashville. It was customary then to exchange letters with your future roommates, and I was so impressed by what I read. They challenged me by example before we even met in person. Each seemed so eager to accomplish something important at Yale. Peter, I remember, wanted to join and eventually head the student paper—and he did. Without their solid and immediate grounding, I certainly would have gone astray. After several years of freely enjoying life in Pomfret's cocoon, I felt rocked by the explosion of numbers on Yale's campus as I entered in the fall of 1952.

My freshman year marked a pivotal moment in Yale's educational philosophy. The spring before I entered, a team of faculty members had engaged in a study that compared Ivy League and preparatory high school curricula. First- and second-year undergraduates had been struggling academically, and professors thought the culprit was boredom, not difficulty. Proving this theory, the study found significant overlaps between high school and undergraduate course content. The university charged professors with realigning their syllabi, and the admissions department became more selective. This was one reason why Yale hesitated at my application. No longer did attendance at Andover and Exeter guarantee a Yale diploma. As a result, the institution became less concentrated with East Coast prep students and more attracted to bright, well-rounded, public school students like my roommates.

Peter, Bob, and Rocky were too far from home to return on every school holiday, so Mother and Bob happily entertained them at our home in New York. I took them to all of my hangouts, including the famous Jimmy Ryan's jazz bar downtown. They held me steady on campus, but back in Manhattan I happily resumed my role as playboy of the western world.

❖ 20 ❖

No amount of studying could keep me from flunking Biology my freshman year. Oh, how I hated that class. At the end of the semester, my adviser called me into his office. To stay off of academic probation, he said, I would need to take a summer class to replace the failing grade. I decided to do it at home in New York at Columbia University. But I'd be damned if I ever entered a Biology lab again. Instead, I enrolled in Archaeology, figuring that one science course was as good as the other.

I loved it. The class was one of my absolute favorites. The banks of the Hudson River are gold mines for archaeologists, and I had a ball doing so much of my coursework outdoors. I got something like a 98 in the class and, once back at Yale, presented the grade happily to my adviser.

He looked grave. "Ted, you failed Biology, not Archaeology," I remember him saying. "You were supposed to take Biology to catch up. Who gave you permission to change?"

"Nobody," I answered. "I just assumed it was a science and I could trade it."

"Don't assume," he said. "When you are given instructions, you are supposed to follow them."

That might have been my first lesson in making assumptions. I would remember it, but in the moment, I was thrilled that I got away with swinging that class credit. Perhaps there was more of Hampton Robb in me than I realized.

ENTERING MY SOPHOMORE YEAR, I HAD NO IDEA WHAT to choose as my major. I had loved Archaeology but knew that science wasn't my bag. It wasn't that I didn't want to take responsibility for my future. I just had no clue what I was going to do. What I loved was socializing. I wanted to major in that.

I joined the Chi Psi fraternity my sophomore or junior year. Known to be the loosest with drinking, Chi Psi got my attention because none of my close associates was pledging there. Soon my fraternity brothers picked me as their entertainment chairman. On weekends I would spend time in downtown New Haven to scout bands to play for parties we hosted after football games.

DAD WOULD COME UP FOR THE HARVARD VERSUS YALE games and sit with me in the student section. I'd see Uncle Ted at the games too, and also my cousin Allan Ryan, the son of Mother's oldest brother. He was two years ahead of me at Yale and I was glad to have him for guidance on occasion. He was the brother of Nancy, who had tried to force my arm into applying to Harvard. Those two didn't get along that well. (Allan would become an investment banker on Wall Street, and Nancy became mixed up with an ashram in Europe. I think I followed the right cousin's advice.)

By sophomore year, I also played intramural football and pick-up basketball, and I swam and played tennis. I even came close to joining the polo team. Somehow the coach there heard that I had played on the junior championship team in Arizona and invited me to try out. Still in love with horses, I almost said yes—and then he told me that each candidate needed his own string of three ponies for tryouts.

I said the only string I had was the one hanging from my suit.

In hindsight, I probably could have met that requirement. Barry was still very much involved with horses on Uncle Ted's Connecticut farm, and I'm sure he could have found three ponies for me. But that caveat just irked me—it took my breath away. What it did was flag the team as a symbol of "wealth incorporated." I wanted no part of that.

EVENTUALLY, I SETTLED ON POLITICAL SCIENCE AS A major and assimilated into Calhoun College. I did fine academically. Interestingly enough, my two favorite classes at Yale had seemingly nothing to do with my major. One wasn't even at Yale. In addition to that summer Archaeology class at Columbia, the other course I found compelling was on Shakespeare. It focused on the playwright's tragedies, and I hadn't thought that much about the history of tragedy.

My richest academic experience came from my senior society's weekly dinners. I was tapped for Book & Snake, the fourth oldest of Yale's secret societies, toward the end of my junior year. So was Gil Chapman, my oldest friend from Pomfret. In addition to him, our delegation was just sensational. Once a week, we would meet in the society's white marble building at the corner of Grove and High streets. Fashioned as a temple in the Classical Greek Revival style, "the Tombs" is set behind a fence decorated with wrought-iron snakes.

Before every meeting, leaders would assign members a topic to consider and prepare remarks on. One person would be selected to share his remarks, then the others would critique and discuss his thoughts. In some ways, this ritual echoed Bob Dentler's eighth-grade composition homework. I'd have to say that in so many ways Dentler prepared me for these important engagements. No single activity proved more preparatory for my professional life than this public speaking practice nurtured by Book & Snake.

⸱ 21 ⸱

L ike all college students through the ages, my classmates and I debated current events and philosophy
late into the night. What was going on in the world
started making inroads into our thought process. In terms
of international events, the Korean War ended in 1953, and
Dwight Eisenhower was serving his first presidential term.
When the president ran for reelection in 1956, both he and
his opponent, Adlai Stevenson, visited campus.

My voice was almost the only Republican one among
my peers. Peter Tomei, a future lawyer, and Rocky Sud-
dath, a future ambassador to Jordan, were strong Democrats and Stevenson supporters. I, of course, supported
Eisenhower. Mother donated significantly to his campaign, as did her brothers.

THREE TOPICS OCCUPIED MOST OF MY COLLEGE CONVER-
sations: women, politics, and religion. I loved talking about
the first, didn't mind talking about the second, and struggled to talk about the third.

Yale didn't have many Catholics, although my roommate Peter Tomei did count as one. The average student was
Protestant or agnostic. When asked how I could believe in
saints and symbols, I never knew what to say. My classmates
didn't ruthlessly mock my faith, but Peter and I would
deflect some barbs.

A journalist and future lawyer, Peter had quite a way with words. He could choose the right ones so quickly. I would stand amazed as he articulated his defense of the faith. I couldn't explain my beliefs nearly as well. That made me feel weak. I would beat myself up repeatedly, telling myself I didn't know enough to stand up to my classmates. Part of me has felt like this all of my life—I would describe it as being half a step behind my other fellow Catholics.

The larger issue was that I didn't really know why I believed what I did. Never had I engaged in an in-depth assessment of religion. I went to church because that's what Mother expected. And I never complained. Something drew me to Mass on Sundays. In New Haven, Peter and I went to St. Thomas More. It was a lovely little church—the door reminded me of the entrance into a speakeasy. Uncle Ted was one of the three founders of this church, having donated a significant amount of money for its construction. Uncle Ted didn't seem particularly religious, but he clearly believed in the presence of Catholicism at Yale.

At Arizona Desert School and Pomfret, being Catholic did make me sensitive to the fact that minorities existed in all parts of life. But I never engaged in conversations with minorities about their differences. This was largely because, other than those who accompanied me to and from church, I had no contact with any. Pomfret didn't have one Black student, and my class at Yale had only two. Yale did have a few Jewish students, and I had at least one good Jewish friend, but religion never came up in our conversations.

Frustrated with my inability to defend my beliefs, I thought that perhaps my classmates were right to doubt

Catholicism and I was in the wrong. I left the church during my freshman year. After attending Mass every Sunday for 19 years, I didn't go to a service for about two years.

Peter Tomei was certainly disappointed.

"You're not as dumb as you think you are," he would say.

Repeatedly, Peter would tell me that I was a good Catholic and that I wasn't doing anyone any good by not attending church. I started listening to him. And I listened more closely to another voice, the one calling me from within. I returned to St. Thomas More during my junior year because I felt something important was missing from my life. Peter was right. My reaction to those probing conversations didn't make any sense. Sitting out from church wasn't solving anything or making me any more educated. I spoke with one of the priests about my concerns, and he recommended some books on church history and apologetics that would help fill gaps in my religious education. I wasn't proud of much of the church history that I read, but I came to understand the reasons for Catholicism. The readings helped me put into words what and why I believed.

I remember having a good talk with my guardian angel when I returned to the church. The conversation emboldened me. I felt confirmation that I was doing the right thing.

⁖ 22 ⁖

The summer after graduation, I took the international trip of a lifetime with Charlie Lord and Sabin Robbins ("Robbie"), two of my best friends. Charlie's mother worked for the United Nations, and as a graduation present, she arranged for the three of us to go on a summer trip throughout Eastern Europe during the Cold War. Each of us had majored in political science. The thought that we could visit East Germany and Moscow, both closed to Americans, was unbelievable.

Mary Pillsbury Lord, an heir to the Pillsbury fortune, was a remarkable woman of her time, as well as a socialite and top Democratic donor. When Charlie and I were sophomores at Yale, President Eisenhower appointed her as the US representative to the UN Commission on Human Rights. She was the second person who held this post: the first was Eleanor Roosevelt, who left to focus on First Lady duties.

According to *The New York Times*, Mary Lord "helped persuade" Gen. Dwight Eisenhower to run for office. She had worked closely with Eleanor Roosevelt during World War II when Mrs. Lord served as the head of women's activities of the National War Fund. Mrs. Lord spearheaded national fundraising for war charities, and as chairman of the Civilian Advisory Committee for the Women's Army Corps, she traveled extensively through Europe. In her UN role, she shaped policies for the National Council of Women, the UN International Children's Emergency Fund, and other organizations. Mrs. Lord went to great effort to mobilize her network so we could take this trip behind the Iron Curtain.

In addition to organizing transportation and recommending a route, Mrs. Lord armed us with various tips, such as how to travel the rails without knowing the languages and how to get the best exchange rates. She cautioned that we would be the first Americans that many nationals would see and that we would be followed by Secret Service agents behind the Iron Curtain. Perhaps most importantly, she told us what to carry should we ever need help—as many packs of Pall Mall cigarettes as possible.

We arrived in Paris in mid-June, then traveled through West and East Germany to Warsaw. It was hard at first to keep up with the various visas and currencies. As we amended parts of our trip, we had to shuffle to adapt Polish visas that were only valid for air travel and East German visas that we could only use for rail travel. We also fumbled with East and West German currencies. We had made a killing on East German marks through the black market but did quite poorly with the West German deutsche mark. Part of the trip's excitement was making some kind of dash to catch the right transportation with the right paperwork at the borders.

We were perhaps most vulnerable in Poland. The very month we arrived in Europe, the Polish people organized massive uprisings against the Communist government of the Polish People's Republic. The center of this unrest was in Poznan, which we were scheduled to travel through.

Thankfully, we made the proper adjustments before leaving Germany. Around 8 p.m. one night, we settled into a first-class compartment with our luggage. As we crossed

Ted Robb

the border, guards threw three people off the train for failing to have the right visas. An overflowing crowd of protesters boarded in Poznan at approximately 2 a.m. Russian guards came with them. Two of these guards entered our compartment and settled among us. I ended up dozing against the shoulder of one.

THE CITY OF WARSAW CONTRASTED SHARPLY WITH THE Parisian lights that started our European journey. Close your eyes for a moment and try to picture the coldest, spartan, austere place you've ever been. That place would look like heaven compared to Warsaw in 1956. Sections of the city looked as if World War II had ended the day before, not in 1944. Drab, heavy, unimaginative-looking buildings emerged from construction sites. The rebuilding was moving quickly, but it was inferior. In the old part of the city, reconstruction tried to copy verbatim historic places that stood before the war. But the masonry looked uneven, and bricks were poorly laid. The State chose to sacrifice quality for the sake of speed.

Evidence of totalitarian control echoed through the empty streets. Loudspeakers lined either side, propaganda placards hung from ruins, and one or two armed men with machine guns stood at major intersections. Any people in sight looked like whipped dogs. I told myself that if I had to live anywhere near Warsaw, I'd go mad.

Dressed in our gray flannel Brooks Brothers clothes, we drew quite a few stares. It made me feel like we were a walking three-ring circus. But although the buildings were off-putting, people were friendly. My camera shocked some. Our guide had to convince one group that it wasn't some type of secret weapon. I felt like a member of royalty among hordes of very unfortunate people.

"It looks as though the people of Poland haven't enjoyed a good laugh in a long while," I wrote in a letter to Mother and Bob Ellinger.

I do remember a rather impressive-looking outdoor sports arena. Athletics were important to the youth. It also was fascinating to see the state's emphasis on reconstructing demolished churches. Two and three churches stood on some blocks. On a Sunday, I noticed overflowing crowds at the modest buildings. It was clear to me that people were there for the sole purpose of worshipping God amid all that had happened. There was hope in this. The church was the one barrier that the Communists couldn't tear down on their march to control the minds and actions of this nation. It seemed the West could have a door into Warsaw through the Catholic Church.

"If Communism is carrying on a war against religion, I can tell you one place in which they're losing the battle—and badly," I wrote. "Let me tell you it's a sight that warms the heart after seeing so much despair and seeming utter hopelessness."

At each stop, Mrs. Lord had arranged for us to meet with ambassadors who seemed only too happy to host us for luncheons and other social events. At the office of Ambassador Joseph Jacobs, we became fast friends with his Marine receptionist. This officer took us to the basement, where we saw an overabundance of American supplies including orange juice, toothpaste, and shaving cream. Fortunately, we could also stock up on cigarettes after giving most of ours away in East Germany. One pack of American cigarettes meant more to these people than their own currency. One US dollar exchanged for four Polish zloty. Each zloty translated to one-hundred grozy. Breakfast cost about five dollars a day, or twenty zloty. The average worker earned three zloty an hour.

One evening, the Canadian delegation hosted us with a party and, on another, we spent two hours in the Soviet-built Palace of Culture and Science. The palace was nothing to look at from the outside, but the indoor view was magnificent. It boasted huge lecture rooms, a concert hall, a stage, swimming pool, and restaurant, and about twenty-five stories of offices. Clearly, life for some in Poland wasn't exactly as it looked walking through Warsaw's streets.

The Polish People's Republic obviously was aware of our presence and tried to use us as propaganda tools. I remember one interview with a reporter on Radio Poland, a propaganda organ.

Another day we were scheduled to have an interview with the director of the Polish Institute of Internal Affairs. Had we thought it was simply a cultural exchange, we were dead wrong. After five minutes, the man said he wanted us to meet his colleagues, and about a dozen "experts" in Communism filed into the room. It was quite a show. I've never heard the Communist line so beautifully defended nor the Americans so skillfully attacked. Overwhelmed by the number of people in the room, we were all quite chagrined that we were not able to make a better showing for the United States. These guys, though, were masters at ducking questions and shifting the trend of discussions the way they wanted.

We had more than one lunch with the American ambassador and his wife. I enjoyed this time, especially as they had a niece who I fell for. The ambassador's wife made sure that we knew secret police might be following us. We noticed their presence at one of the athletic arenas. They followed us when the ambassador accompanied us to a football game between Egypt and Poland. Boy, did I embarrass that man when I rooted for the wrong team by accident.

Our Marine friend led us around a few evenings. At one party sponsored by the French Embassy at a night-club, we met diplomats from every embassy in Warsaw. We also met several of this Marine's fellow servicemen stationed at the embassy.

"If ever you're interested where the taxpayers' money goes," I wrote to Mother and Bob Ellinger after one evening with the Marines, "let me say you helped pay for dinner tonight—steak a la USA, strawberry shortcake, and our first martinis since Paris."

⁙ 23 ⁙

A large delegation met our plane in Moscow. We were quite impressed with ourselves before we realized they weren't there to greet us but Dutch newsmen on the flight.

Moscow—our most highly anticipated stop—was interesting but didn't end up being the highlight of the trip. We visited the Kremlin and saw its treasures of the tsars. We saw Russian Orthodox churches that had been converted into museums, and we went to an agricultural fair described to us as the "World's Fair of Soviet Nationalities," a place meant to impress visitors and give the Russian people a feeling of pride. The only thing that impressed me at the Tretyakov, the national art gallery, was the crowds. Except for a few, the artworks seemed very unimaginative and were poorly hung. Every other room held a bust or portrait of Lenin. The museum boasted no abstract or modern art, with an entire section devoted to anti-German propaganda.

The largest crowds we saw were outside the tombs of Stalin and Lenin. Each had a line two to three blocks long. Inside, the atmosphere resembled that of a church. The people's reverence for these resting places felt overwhelming. I didn't dare whip out my camera for fear that I might be strung up by five Russian guards and run out of town by the local Moscow gentry.

The American ambassador to Russia knew Uncle Ted quite well. Secretary of State John Foster Dulles had appointed Charles E. Bohlen, a Foreign Services veteran, to that position at the start of the Eisenhower administration. When the House passed the nomination 15-0, Senator Joseph McCarthy vehemently fought what he called a "tremendous mistake," all but accusing Bohlen of being a Soviet spy. "Unless Mr. McCarthy can demonstrate that Mr. Bohlen is a Russian spy, or that he once burned down an orphan asylum, the Senate will undoubtedly give the nomination a heavy majority," wrote *The New York Times.* Fortunately, the Senate recognized the truth in this statement. Bohlen, a career diplomat and Soviet Union specialist fluent in Russian, was the perfect choice to serve American interests in the nucleus of the Cold War.

We met Ambassador Bohlen first in his office. Pulling us to one side, he pointed to the American seal. He wanted us to know that the Russians had bugged it, but Bohlen's team left the microphones, not wanting them to realize that the Americans knew. His point was well taken, but the notion that Russians would bug such a symbol of American liberty shocked me. I've never forgotten that.

Bohlen's wife was a delightful hostess, securing invitations for us to quite a few events. At one—perhaps a British armed forces attaché party where we met diplomatic corps from many nations—I fell again for someone's niece. This woman's uncle was the ambassador from Iceland of all places.

I made it a point to attempt to understand the place of the church (particularly the Catholic Church) everywhere we visited. In Moscow I saw only one Roman Catholic church, and it was in very poor condition. A conversation with our Russian guide about religion turned into a heated argument on her end. She stated that since her history books never mentioned any saints, she didn't believe in religion. And because she had never seen God, she couldn't believe in him. Her dogmatic approach to the discussion was something to behold.

Many would have disagreed with her in Zagorsk, a town outside Moscow. Mobs of peasants filled Zagorsk streets for the religious festival of St. George. Next to a visiting group of British clergy, we Americans were the number one attraction. People followed us everywhere. Handing us autographed postcards to take home, they asked us if we liked Moscow and whether we thought there would be another war.

One group we most definitely avoided was a set of American tourists. One young man opened his coat to reveal an American flag sewn into his lapel. He had another flag draped over his camera. It was awful. In the midst of another culture's religious festival, in another country, he whipped out two postcard folders of Los Angeles and waved them in front of peasants in a haughty fashion.

The religious fervor from the crowd did make an impression on me. One man made the mistake of crossing himself outside of the church. That was apparently against the law, and police fined him twenty-five rubles. This image, in particular, made an interesting commentary on the people's democracy.

⁑ 24 ⁑

fter a visit to the ambassador's country home, we took a night sleeper train to Leningrad. Once again, we made fast friends with a group of Marines at the embassy who entertained us well. In both Moscow and Leningrad, the food was better and more plentiful. Every night we had vodka and caviar.

"I'm becoming fast convinced that next to the ambassadors, the best people to meet and to get to know in these foreign countries are the Marines," I wrote home. "I'm also beginning to feel like the world's number one sponge, but I'm not complaining."

With its network of winding canals, Leningrad reminded me of Amsterdam, only without the bicycles. It was a welcome change after Moscow. The entire spirit of the city was more alive and gay, even though a good bit of destruction from the 900-day siege remained and propaganda loomed everywhere. At the Hermitage Gallery, I saw one of the greatest collections of French Impressionist paintings that I had seen up to that time. I found it more impressive than the Louvre. Overall, the architecture of Leningrad was less oppressive than that of Moscow.

Once again, the city was perhaps most impressive underground. The subway system looked like the inside of a palace, heavily ornamented. Each station appeared as eye-catching and clean as a room at Versailles. Sabin Robbins and I said that more people should host parties in Soviet subways. We came up with a theory as to why the government spent so much money underground: It hoped the main transportation system would serve as a psychological lift to the Russian people.

Above and below ground, curious crowds followed us. The streets were extremely wide and very crowded. More people took risks jaywalking in Leningrad than in Manhattan. Two things in particular surprised us on the streets— English speakers and female construction workers. Because students had to study English in school, many young people spoke it surprisingly well. And at almost every construction site, women laborers outnumbered men. Women appeared to have all of the unpleasant jobs, including street cleaning.

In the city center, one museum full of antireligious propaganda loomed larger than life. Although I counted about eighteen "working" churches in town, I wrote home that religion seemed nonexistent. I did attend Mass one Sunday at a Catholic church packed with Dutch sailors. These men, also surrounded by locals wherever they walked, figured prominently in the nightlife. Perched aboard their anchored ships, they would serenade Leningrad with Dutch songs in the evenings. Russians on the street would sing back to them. It was quite a spectacle.

⁙ 25 ⁙

Bucharest, I later wrote, was the most interesting and exciting stop to date. Of all the countries we visited, Romania was the one that had begun pulling away from Soviet control first. Younger Romanians, such as our tour guide, spoke more freely against Communist control than anyone we had yet encountered. Older Romanians seemed caught between the old and new worlds. Many of this generation spoke French but saw it as a liability, evidence of a life that preceded and thus threatened Communist control.

Compared to Warsaw, Bucharest had more life but fewer cars moving through its streets. Housing was quite crowded, and prices were fantastically high. Orchestras provided entertainment for outdoor restaurants, but only wealthy tourists like us could afford to eat there. We mingled among visitors from other Eastern European countries on so-called cultural delegations, but we were among the first Americans to visit Romania in about twenty years.

As a result, our hotel most probably was wired and the ambassador told us that secret police would follow us everywhere.

Our guide was beautiful. She also was outspoken on her political views. One morning we had a new guide, an older woman who appeared out of the Stone Age. Perhaps the tourist agency had pulled the younger woman because she spoke out against the state. Or perhaps they learned that she had spent one evening in the arms of Sabin Robbins, that lady killer.

The chief minister in Romania turned out to be a classmate of Uncle Phil's at Harvard. He escorted us to an American propaganda film one evening and then to the beach for a few days. The weather had been cool and damp until we reached Romania, when the days turned quite hot. We all wanted to go for a dip in the Black Sea but nobody had packed a bathing suit. Fortunately, we could rent them. Unfortunately, we could only find Speedos (we called them bikinis).

On the beach, we had many conversations with people our age who freely expressed their postwar dissatisfaction. We found their pessimistic views of America fairly astounding. Despite the free speech, an atmosphere of distrust surrounded us. The whole country seemed blanketed in paranoia. Nobody trusted the next person, and those who aired their complaints to the wrong people knew they were liable to end up behind bars or, in some cases, in front of an extermination squad. In one conversation, it took us fifteen minutes to convince a group that we were not members of the Securitate looking to ensnare protesters.

Our Romanian experience taught us that we could study all we wanted about totalitarian governments and societies run by fear, but until we saw them in operation, we had no idea of their terrifying effect on free speech.

On our final day in Bucharest, we had three interviews scheduled with the press. During the first two, reporters tried their best to put words in our mouths. We gave noncommittal, polite answers, aware that they were trying their damnedest to use us as propaganda. Told that we could ask the reporters questions, we found that they only gave the party line.

The chief US minister said that since we were leaving that night, it would be okay to present a more challenging interview on our third go-round. He wanted to make sure that the American image didn't look too weak. Sabin and I had carefully worked out a set of questions should we be given this opportunity, and we went all out. The journalist maintained a straight face, unwilling and unable to argue with us.

Once again we felt like celebrities with all of these interviews and photographs. The government had a carefully laid plan to impress us half to death. But you never cover up what lies beneath the surface. Especially when you hear the voices of people who refuse to be indoctrinated and who refuse to join the syncopated symphony of the Communist line.

☙ 26 ☙

The train trip from Bucharest to Belgrade was one of the wildest rides of my life.

We left the station one evening at 10 p.m. and slept well. Late the following morning at a stop in Romania, I asked a conductor in French how much time we might have to grab a bite to eat as there was no dining car onboard. It sounded like he said thirty-five minutes. Leaving the sleeping Robbins in the train car, Charlie Lord and I rushed to get some food along with one other person. Barry Farrell, one of our Yale professors, was writing a book about Eastern Europe when he heard about our trip. Asking to join us, he accompanied us on certain stops and traveled elsewhere on others.

Lord and Farrell put me in charge of watching the track in case the train took off early. Suddenly I sensed movement. I realized that I was paying attention to the last two cars, which had been detached at the station. Shuffling forward, I watched the train—with Robbins, our luggage, and most of our money—heading down the tracks.

Holding hot food in our sweaty hands, we rushed to the station master's office, where Charlie and I pulled enough French together to get some help. Someone mobilized the phones and sent telegrams to stop the train before it reached the Yugoslavia border about fifty kilometers away. But we had to find a way to get to the train. And it would only wait a certain amount of time before starting again.

Nobody wanted to drive us as the roads were terrible. Plus, all of our Romanian money had been spent, and because it was a Sunday, there wasn't any place open to cash American Express checks. We also didn't have enough cigarettes to bargain with.

Fortunately, Charlie had American dollars on him. It took about twenty-five minutes of haggling, begging, and almost screaming, but finally we convinced a cab driver to take us to the train. He wanted fifty dollars and we were in no position to argue. By then probably half the town surrounded us. Trying to dissuade attention, we handed out the cigarettes we had left. They made us so popular that we could have made a run for mayor.

The driver did get us to the train on time. Once there he demanded more than the fifty dollars agreed upon. I argued with him in French, but he pretended not to understand me as he didn't want customs officials to know he spoke the language. I sought the help of one of these agents, who promptly confiscated all the American money the cab driver held. As our train pulled away, the cab driver stood on the platform cursing at us in German and Romanian.

Ted Robb

⁙ 27 ⁙

I was in Belgrade when I received word from the embassy that my father had died. He was sixty-one.

I had known that Dad was quite ill. He and Gertie had moved to La Jolla, California, when I started at Yale largely because both were in poor health. She died about a year or so before he did.

Dad was so distraught after Gertie's death that he was in no position to organize a funeral for her. I remember accompanying him and her body to Colorado, where she was from. Fortunately, the summer before Gertie died, I had spent time in Aspen working as a hotel bellboy with a Yale classmate (one of the greatest jobs I have ever had). This same classmate was able to assist me in funeral plans for Gertie. With his help, I ran that entire funeral. I did all of that out of love for Dad. I never liked Gertie. My cousins remember her as someone fun who laughed a lot, and maybe that's why Dad loved her like he did. As soon as she died, his health took a plunge.

I saw Dad between graduating from Yale and leaving for Eastern Europe. He suffered from lung disease and had a terrible time breathing. He looked horrible. I can't emphasize how attractive the man once was. He could charm the birds off the tree. Despite his appearance, that last visit held something special for both of us. It was then that we had our first real conversation as father and son. Perhaps he had premonitions of his death. I know that I sensed it.

I thought about staying home from my European trip in the event that Dad died that summer. I even spoke to Mother about it. I decided to go, though, because that final conversation had meant something. I've always struggled with attending funerals. I'd much rather remember people as they were when they were alive. I knew that Dad wouldn't want me to give up this European trip of a lifetime. When I left, I told myself I wasn't coming back for any funeral.

That's what I told the embassy in Belgrade when asked if I needed help making arrangements. Mother respected my decision, but my two older half-sisters had a hard time with it. Elizabeth in particular was furious with me. She lived in Cincinnati and made the arrangements for Dad's funeral in Cleveland. Elizabeth couldn't believe that I wouldn't come home for Dad when I had done so much for Gertie. But I knew her feelings were more complicated than that. Dad had left when she and Roberta were little girls, and at the moment of his death, Elizabeth was in the beginning stages of divorce. A few different things fueled her anger. We talked it out later, but I don't think Elizabeth ever forgave me.

Needing to process my thoughts, I wrote a letter to Mother. It was my way of attending Dad's funeral. In some ways, it was a letter to her and to him. When I read it now, it feels final in some way.

⁖ 28 ⁖

Hotel Palace—Belgrade

AUGUST 9, 1956

Dear Mother,

The news reached me the other day of the old man's death, and I guess now is as good a time as any to get a number of things off my chest—things I've wanted to say before now but never could really express them as I wanted. Before I get going however I want you to know—and I hope you already do—that I love you very much—and regardless of what I may say in this letter it still holds very true.

Dad and I never established a true father-son relationship—and perhaps this was more my fault than anyone else's. To me he meant nothing more than an extremely enjoyable summer visit. I think we met for the first time as true father and son last winter when I went out to see him. For when I came back I knew I had met a great guy, and I sincerely regretted that we had not been able to become close friends sooner than we had.

Before I go any further I want you to know that I consider myself a very fortunate young man to be the son of two such fine people—and to have spent twenty-two great years made possible only by numerous sacrifices on your part. It's more than education—numerous trips to Europe—clothes that I'm thankful for—those are only the tangible bits of evidence that one has led a comfortable and enjoyable life. It goes much deeper than that, deeper perhaps that I lack the proper words to it,—call it a way of life—a foundation, a preparedness to face whatever the future offers—it is for these things that I am eternally thankful.

Perhaps the one thing I missed however, more than any other thing thus far was being a part of a mother-father team. I missed it because I know now you two are among the truly fine people to have ever come along. To be your son was an honor—to have been a member of a family team composed of you and dad would have been a privilege. I never asked why this was not possible, and I frankly think I don't ever want to know. I feel somehow that you two never really broke apart—for there was a great love between you even though you were not together. Neither of you ever spoke a harsh word one about the other at least in my presence. For that I am most grateful, for otherwise I might be a completely different person now—torn between two persons.

You have led your life as you have seen fit, and I am certainly not qualified to pass judgment on it nor is that my aim in this letter. Rather I am recording some sentiments which I have kept bottled up for some time now—sentiments that I would like to share with you as my mother.

At this point I would like to mention Bob, and how he fits into the bond that binds us Robbs together—you, dad and myself. As a stepfather, they don't make them any better. As a friend and as someone to rely on he has proven himself beyond a question of a doubt. With dad gone—I will rely on Bob for any question or problem ordinarily asked of a father and at the same time accord him the same respect I would my own father. I feel very lucky that I have Bob to rely on because next to dad I know of no one else who I respect more, and among the older generations I consider him my best friend. You and I both have a lot to be thankful for that Bob is around to help guide us.

Last Sunday you and I both lost someone we loved—but life must go on. I only hope that I can make you as proud of me as I am, to be your son— the son of two of the finest people I've ever known.
Love,
Ted

I clearly chose to get a few things off my chest with this letter. But I didn't intend for my disclosures to open new doors in our relationship. If anything, they closed some conversations before they could begin.

The letter provided closure not just for my father's death but also for what I had always longed for as a child: a traditional family. It was my way of saying a lot of things to my mother that I had never said before. The act of writing was to acknowledge my dad, but also to let her know how I saw his place in my life. In that way, it was an act of respect. When I returned home two months later, she told me that the letter had meant a great deal. I think she was shocked that I would sit down and write something like that to her.

That night, I told Robbins, Lord, and Farrell that Dad had died. None of them had known that he was very ill. I spoke with them then about my childhood. Rarely had I talked to anybody about it before. I don't think it was until I had to give a personal biography at Book & Snake that I had shared anything about my parents' separation. Perhaps that was because I didn't quite know what to make of Dad's place in my life. It wasn't until he pulled that act at the Harvard Club that I realized how much he thought about me.

Rereading this letter today, I hear myself saying one thing that I didn't write:

"Oh, would that we would have been."

❖ 29 ❖

B elgrade resembled Paris after our other stops. Yugoslavia had a history of entertaining the Allied and Axis forces together. The air about the city was more refined, gayer, and lighter. Sidewalk cafes sprinkled the town. Stores appeared brighter. Restaurants appeared attractive and had much more reasonable prices. This atmosphere was reflected in the faces of Belgrade's people—they seemed happier and more frank in their discussions, less worried about retaliation from eavesdropping ears.

Our reception there was fantastic, and Farrell, who was writing a book about Belgrade among other topics, was on cloud nine. Among our hosts were the American minister and his embassy staff, and we also had two visits with the Indian ambassador and his wife. Sporting events occupied much of our time. We were there to see the running of the "Tito" cup, Belgrade's version of the Kentucky Derby, and almost got caught in a near riot when the finish was disputed. (We also lost a good amount of money gambling against the winner.) There was another disputed decision and near riot after a boxing match between Yugoslavia and Czechoslovakia.

In Belgrade we had eleven interviews with various groups. Farrell made us quite proud with a speech he gave to the Institute of Economic and Political Affairs. After several weeks trekking around Eastern Europe with the man, we had almost forgotten he was a renowned Yale professor.

⁑ 30 ⁑

From Belgrade we stopped in Vienna before flying to Prague. Vienna was quiet. Much of the war damage had disappeared. We ran into more American tourists there than anywhere else, and I wrote home that the nationals seemed happy. I couldn't help thinking, though, that they sought something more from life.

"One thing this trip has pointed out clearly is the advantage of a solid, good education," I wrote. "There is no substitute, though God knows the people behind the curtain are searching for one." In Vienna, I had time to reflect on our whole trip. More than anything else, the trip had taught me that there was no perfect form of government. I had come to appreciate and understand the American system more, shortcomings and all.

From Prague, we would reenter West Germany before splitting up. Robbie and Farrell would head for Rotterdam and a ship home, and Charlie Lord and I would visit Paris again before heading to London.

Farrell had gone ahead to Prague. A couple of days before leaving Vienna, we wired the local tourist agency there of when and where we would be arriving so it could send transportation. I signed it with our last names—Lord Robb Robbins. Upon arrival at the airport, a very well-dressed man waited at the gate to meet a "Mr. Robbins." He seemed surprised that there were three in our party. The man led us to a limousine, which in turn surprised us. We largely traveled through and in "C-level" accommodations. Soon it delivered us to a hotel. But it wasn't the hotel that was on our itinerary, the one where Farrell awaited our arrival. This hotel was splendid, glamorous, and clearly meant for A-listers. Wondering what had happened, we took a cab to the correct hotel, where a very haggard and frazzled Farrell welcomed us with open arms. He thought we had been kidnapped.

When we hadn't arrived, Farrell had called the airline terminal and learned that a well-dressed man had approached us. Then he heard we had followed the man into a limousine. Farrell was beside himself until he saw us walking toward him. Together we figured out what had happened—the tourism company thought that Lord Robb Robbins was an actual lord, one person deserving of the finest accommodations. Others had figured out the mistake as well. By the time we returned to the A-level hotel to get our bags, the concierge had thrown them into the street.

In a Prague nightclub, we befriended an American visiting his family. A woman with him was the mother of the bandleader, and after the show, she introduced us to the musicians. The bandleader invited us to dinner one evening at his home.

The musician's wife and her mother cooked a delicious meal, and over conversation, we learned that before the war, they had lived wealthy lives. Now they lived together in a crowded three-room apartment. He told us that all bands were required to play four Czech songs before anything else. It was amusing to return to the nightclub after we heard that. We could see how the band tore through those pieces quickly, receiving no attention from the loud audience eating their dinners. But as soon as that fourth song ended and American songs began, everyone took to the dance floor. The bandleader begged us to send all sorts of American records to him.

This was a common request. Nationals often asked us to mail things to them, and we agreed to do so. When I returned home I knew to ask about this. I was told no. Packages from America, I learned, could cast suspicion on our friends.

⁙ 31 ⁙

We all sighed with relief when we reentered West Berlin and the Iron Curtain closed tightly behind us. While we wouldn't have traded the trip for anything, it felt good to be back on free soil.

"One thing I can tell you for sure," I wrote home, "is that the US has friends behind that imposing curtain—only what can we do for them?"

Although the Berlin Wall would not be constructed until 1962, for all intents and purposes it already was there. Natural barriers and very tall watchtowers marked the border between east and west. The East German regime made it clear in other ways that they didn't want their citizens infected by democracy. It was as if there were a huge sign posted that said, "Stay away from us." The wall would only become the physical presence of what had been understood.

My initial relief was short-lived. Almost as soon as we arrived in West Germany, Robbins and I decided to try getting East German visas so that we could see Dresden. Charlie declined. He said he didn't want to risk prison.

We had East German visas before, but they didn't allow for return visits; each had very specific dates—even approved hours—of travel marked on them. Mrs. Lord had gone to such trouble to arrange this trip that we wanted to do everything we could to make her proud. Should there have been a problem or some unaddressed suspicion with our visa request, we could have ended up in some kind of detention. But we got them.

Dresden was so decimated that the old center of town was nothing more than a field on which stood a few daisies and some brick reminders of former buildings. The old main shopping street consisted of nothing but skeleton structures with all the insides burned out. Reconstruction was moving at a snail's pace, especially compared to West German cities like Munich.

Robbins and I loved our guide, who met us at the station, sat with us at dinner, and later took us home to meet his wife. They served us a creamy-looking liquor called Eitr that was the best thing I had ever tasted. What those two told us was enough to turn our hair gray. They lived fairly comfortably, but to do so, they both worked twelve to fourteen-hour days. While they relished the opportunity to host us, their complaints were numerous. They didn't move to the western sector, the man said, because of the astronomical exchange rate: four East German marks to one West German mark. Asked about the present regime, he said, "If you've got enough money you can bear the rest."

Our guide had joined the German army at sixteen and spent the majority of his life fighting or suffering the consequences of war. A prisoner of war during World War II, he was freed from an American camp only to return home and find that he had to live in a similar system for the rest of his life. There had been hope for change in 1953 during the Berlin uprising in the eastern zone, but then resignation had set in. Both said they were tired of fighting. Resigned to their situation, they spent all of their time working to have enough money to live as well as they could.

Leaving him and his wife was entirely frustrating. We saw them as terribly young in spirit. When our guide put us on the train to Berlin, he refused to let us pay what we owed him. All we could do was say we would send him two packs of Pall Mall cigarettes, a small recompense for his kindness.

⁖ 32 ⁖

At the end of August, Robbins and Farrell sailed from Rotterdam and Charlie Lord and I spent three more weeks on our adventure. We spent some time in Munich and then a week and a half or so in London before leaving from Paris on the 19th. The Paris nightlife had cost us so much money upon our arrival in Europe that we didn't dare tempt ourselves with too many more pleasures.

By the time I arrived home in late September, many of my Yale classmates were in the first months of their professional careers. Mother and Bob Ellinger very much wanted me to find a job on Wall Street. I couldn't have been less interested in that path.

I hadn't thought much about my career while on the European trip. Sabin Robbins was headed for graduate school at Oxford (before finding a career in zoo management), and Charlie Lord eventually moved to the Washington, DC, area, where he established himself as a headmaster at girls' schools. But with a Yale degree and all the connections and resources in the world, I had no real direction. I could very well have spent more years going to Yale football games and fraternity parties.

The best thing to do, I decided, was to enter the Navy. I signed up for Officer Candidate School in Newport, Rhode Island. If nothing else, military service would give me time to figure out what I really wanted to do. By the time I entered OCS the following spring, I had another person to consider as I planned for the future.

⸱ 33 ⸱

Fairly soon after I had returned from Eastern Europe, two FBI agents paid me a visit at home. I had no idea what they wanted but invited them inside. After a question or two, I soon realized that the agents were assessing whether I was a Communist sympathizer. Apparently, my trip had raised a red flag. I said I was on a cultural visit arranged by Mrs. Lord at the UN for me and two other Yale graduates. I don't know what these men believed, but they sure asked a lot of questions. They didn't scare me. More than anything, I felt stunned that anyone would challenge my loyalty to America.

I talked to the Lords about it later, and they weren't surprised. Charlie never received such a visit, probably because of his mother's work. When I think about it now, I realize a several factors could have turned the FBI onto our visit. It was the era of the Red Scare, and Senator Joseph McCarthy had implied on numerous occasions that Ambassador Bohlen had Communist sympathies. We had very much enjoyed the company of Bohlen and his wife. Perhaps it wasn't just the Soviets bugging the seal in his office.

Our Yale group also had made many headlines throughout the Communist Bloc, with Charlie, Sabin, and I being interviewed and photographed to excess. American agents overseas could have flagged us. Another thought is that perhaps one of our Yale classmates shared our trip with his co-workers. Hollywood had glamorized the Ivy League as a platform for government intelligence recruitment in that particular era, and there was some truth to this narrative. Our trip was no secret to our greater school community.

My favorite story of an FBI visit to 79th and Lexington, though, occurred several months later. At Newport, I made an application to read secret documents because of my aspiration to enter military intelligence. I needed to include references on my application, and one of the names I wrote down was "Miriam Ellinger." I didn't state that she was my mother.

Mother soon told me that the FBI had interviewed her. Not anticipating their visit, she had invited them inside and spent a good amount of time answering a series of questions about me. At no point did she tell them that I was her son. They didn't seem to make the connection.

So much for government intelligence.

∻ 34 ∻

Between college graduation and our trip to Europe, Charlie Lord and I became involved in NYC's chapter of Youth for Eisenhower. Upon our return, we reentered campaign work for the month or so remaining before the November 1956 election.

This was, of course, Dwight D. Eisenhower's second campaign. The president and his opponent, Adlai Stevenson, had visited Yale with their stump speeches, and there was something so much more galvanizing about Ike. A well-respected war general, he came across like a grandfather—a strong yet caring leader who had things under control. He was the ideal candidate for the Republican Party at that time. There was more to dislike about Vice President Richard Nixon. Most Ike supporters I knew shared a concern about Nixon's personality. Something about him seemed not so clean-cut.

I was mostly apolitical before joining the campaign. As my friend and classmate Tersh Boasberg says now, politics was a "vanilla" issue on Yale's campus in the mid-1950s. Even my roommates, whom I would have called committed Democrats at the time, didn't come across as "ideologically strong." Abortion was beginning to become an issue, but I don't remember many other pressing hot topics of conversation among our group.

Mother was a very strong and generous supporter of Dwight Eisenhower, and, of course, Charlie Lord's mother had worked closely with the First Lady for over a decade. It was Mother, I think, who encouraged my involvement. Either she or maybe Uncle Ted—still a Connecticut senator—put me in touch with a man who helped run Youth for Eisenhower/Nixon. His name was Dan Ruge, and he was a wonderful guy. He worked as a lawyer and was somehow associated with Nelson Rockefeller, who would become a Republican front-runner in the 1964 election and a future vice president. Ruge immediately plugged me and Charlie Lord into mobilizing the vote.

And that's how I met Margaret Mary Armstrong.

Nobody in Peg's family could believe that she supported Eisenhower. Raised as a Democrat, she was quite outspoken politically. But there was something about Ike that she liked—perhaps that strong grandfatherly quality. Peg's parents had both died during her childhood, and she spent her teenage years living with an aunt and uncle who really didn't want to provide for her. Her two older brothers ended up in jail for misdemeanors, and her only other sibling was a much younger brother.

When she graduated high school, Peg had desperately wanted to go to college, but her aunt and uncle dismissed the possibility.

"We've gone as far as we can go," they told her. "You better find a job because women in the first place don't need to go to college."

Peg left their house as soon as possible. She moved in with her good friend Rosemary ("Posey") Fay, and soon the Fays became a second family to her. Rosemary's mother was a Democratic ward leader, so the household didn't much entertain conversations about women's limitations. Peg found a job after high school as a secretary and worked her way up the corporate ladder, eventually becoming the administrative assistant for a company's vice president of international affairs. Peg's boss had encouraged her campaign involvement. He thought it would be good for the firm. She started volunteering an hour a day, and before long, she was on leave from work as the head of the city's chapter of Youth for Eisenhower/Nixon.

By the time I met her at a meeting, Peg was in her mid-twenties and had been supporting herself for several years. I, on the other hand, had worked only for a couple of months two years before as an Aspen hotel bellhop.

I can't say that sparks flew between us at first. I could tell she knew I had no idea what to do with my life. Having met me when I first graduated from Yale, Peg couldn't believe that I was heading to Europe for three months. She wasn't too impressed with any adventures I might have behind the Iron Curtain.

"Aren't you going to lose an opportunity for work?" she asked me. She thought I was a complete yo-yo with a silver spoon in his mouth. By the time I came back, I told her I was going to join the military. I looked forward to it. I knew I had played for long enough.

⁙ 35 ⁙

The main politicking job that Charlie and I had was driving through the city and registering people to vote. Drivers had to follow strict rules. We couldn't just wander to a certain neighborhood and talk up Ike—each destination had to be preapproved. And while we could decorate the car, we could not designate our affiliation anywhere on it. Our direction was to get people to vote, not just to vote for Eisenhower. There also were regulations on where we could blare soundtracks from the car's loudspeakers.

In addition to destinations, we submitted plans for our routes through the city and our arrival and departure times. We couldn't spend more than fifteen minutes in one particular space. By and large, we were in business districts and not residential neighborhoods. At every stop, Charlie and I would park the car, take our clipboards, and stroll the streets.

We couldn't believe what people would say. Repeatedly people told us that they had better things to do on Election Day. Again and again we would hear, "Why should I vote? My vote doesn't count." A whole swath of people told us not to go to the polls. My youthful enthusiasm was drowned quite a few times by a category of people not interested in democracy.

"Why would you ever NOT use a right?" I would ask.

When I started having these conversations, I wasn't yet old enough to vote. I didn't turn twenty-one until the end of May 1956. But the more I talked to people about the importance of voting, the more desperate I became to vote that fall. Never have I missed an opportunity to vote since—even when I've been less than thrilled with the choice of candidates. To this day, I see voting as an unparalleled right in our democracy, a true opportunity to have one's voice heard.

⁌ 36 ⁍

Peg and I never agreed at committee meetings. I remember one particular disagreement we had over campaigning at churches. Someone suggested having teams waiting on the street on Sunday mornings. As houses of worship dismissed, the thinking went, volunteers could be waiting with campaign literature. Peg thought it was a good idea.

"I really dislike it entirely," I said. "We shouldn't do that."

She tried to ignore me as best she could. I don't think it was that she didn't like me, she just would think, "Who is this guy? A grown college graduate without a job?"

Of course, there were others like me and Charlie, men and women finished with college and awaiting their next chapters. But something about me irked Peg. Probably gall. I had no idea how to run a campaign. I would challenge her at meetings with any passing thought that came through my head. I wasn't shy in the least. Not everyone agreed with her, but most of the time she carried the day.

I got to her once when she sent the most annoying friend of hers, a redhead, along with me on the Ike truck. Peg would have all of her female friends volunteer in this capacity. The Ike truck followed a softer set of regulations than the voter registration cars. This was a clear propaganda vehicle. We would park it on street corners, once again for fifteen minutes at a time, and do whatever we could to attract crowds. We put pictures on tables and blared Ike speeches and patriotic music from loudspeakers. We handed out literature and took pictures of pedestrians standing next to Ike cardboard cutouts. It was a blast. Most of the time.

I had a ball with everyone Peg sent my way...except this particular friend. The woman just talked and talked. The sound of her voice irritated me to no end. I told Peg as much on the phone the following day.

"All the volunteers you've sent to help are sensational," I said, "but the girl last night with the red hair was impossible."

"You'll take who I send and like it!" she exclaimed. Then she slammed the phone down.

I gasped. Nobody had talked to me like that before.

ONCE IN A WHILE, PEG AND I WORKED TOGETHER ON something specific. I remember her setting up a meeting with a very important potential donor who she wanted me to meet—probably an acquaintance of Mother's or Uncle Ted's. We hailed a cab downtown and headed toward 125th Street. But in the middle of a conversation, she glanced at her watch and realized she had double-booked herself.

"Okay, you're off now!" she said. She told the cab to pull over, and she jumped out to head back to the office. Boy, did she leave me high and dry. I was shocked. Then angry. Then impressed that this woman was so important that she had two things to do at once.

I DIDN'T MAKE MY MOVE UNTIL ELECTION NIGHT. IKE took New York City pretty easily, and several of us milled around the campaign office to hear the official results. Peg and I were the last two there around 2 a.m.

I asked if I could give her a lift home.

"That would be very nice," she answered.

In the backseat of the taxi, I wondered if I could get her to say yes to anything else. We were heading to a part of the Lower East Side that I had never been to before.

I remember thinking, "You know, this is probably the last time you are going to see this woman because we have such different backgrounds."

I knew where she worked and could show up at her office, but there was no reason to do so other than to see her. I decided to see if she would have lunch with me. We had disagreed so heartily so often that I knew the answer might not be positive.

She said yes. I called her up soon, and we had a wonderful time. That led to another lunch date, then another and another. With each date I was becoming more and more interested. At some point before I went to Newport, I told Mother that I might marry this woman.

Mother's response dumbfounded me. She was shocked. The two women had met at a political event, and Mother had respected Peg's role in committee work, but she never had thought of her as a future daughter-in-law. Mother's plan had been for me to marry one of the debutantes from the social register. Never in a million years had I thought that she would have a problem with Peg.

Mother said I was moving too fast. She said Peg was from a completely different background. The more she thought about it, the more worked up she became. Soon two of her brothers contacted me. Mother had asked my uncles to talk me out of the idea.

Uncle Peter took me to the Yale Club for lunch. He expressed Mother's concern, but he didn't have a problem with Peg. My cousin Cynthia remembers his and my Aunt Anne's approval, in fact. Uncle Ted was more to the point. The undercurrent of his conversation implied that Peggy might be out to score some financial gain for herself.

Here was a woman who had been employed for years, risen to the top of her field, and organized a significant piece of Dwight Eisenhower's campaign. I had barely worked a day in my life. They should have been concerned about how I was planning to support a family. But that didn't even come up. In the ensuing months before the wedding, Mother and Bob would say that I had "better choices." They said I should wait and not jump into marriage. They said they were concerned that I was getting married simply because it was time to get married. Peg's saving grace with Mother and her brothers was that she was a devout Catholic girl. They certainly couldn't quarrel with that.

At some point during our courting days, I took Peg to meet Uncle Phil and the Robbs in Canada. He, Aunt Mary, and my cousins adored her. There was no question in their minds that Peg was a catch. Nobody there worried about her background.

I knew that Mother was infuriated because I was interested in someone so completely different from what she had envisioned. Peg was from a different mold than any other girl I had ever met. She couldn't be controlled. This became very apparent during the wedding planning. Mother had wanted to plan the wedding of *her* dreams, I'm sure—after all, she had four ceremonies of her own and none was a traditional affair. Peg, though, would have none of that. She barely had any money, but she insisted that she, and not Mother, would plan and pay for the wedding.

I admired Peg's resolve. Yet this made life difficult.

⁚ 37 ⁚

During my time in Eastern Europe, I thought an ideal job for me would be ambassador to France. I adored every moment I had with the diplomatic corps, and my French had become very good. The experience led me to try my hand at entering the Foreign Service. I took a test to start the process when I came home but never followed up on it. I don't know why. It may be that I wanted to protect myself from the draft. There was talk at the time of reinstating it, and entering Officer Candidate School was one way to control any military future I might have.

I signed up for OCS, which combined basic and officer training in a twelve-week course for college graduates, at a naval recruitment office in Manhattan. I told the recruiter right away that I wanted to be assigned to military intelligence because I had traveled so widely. He kind of smirked.

"We're just here to get you into the Navy. Express yourself in Newport."

I don't think many enlisted men showed up and said they wanted to file immediately for top military clearances, which is essentially what I had done. But I knew that I had a shot at that path, largely due to the opportunities that Mrs. Lord's trip to Eastern Europe gave me.

During my twelve weeks in Newport, Rhode Island, I held my breath and waited to get my commission. The Navy aimed to prepare us to be officers on ships' decks wherever we went. I remember talks about ships and orders of command but not much else. Peg visited on the weekends, and occasionally I would see Mother and Bob in Connecticut. They didn't know what to do with me and my white uniform. Bob used to tease that I would end up scrubbing decks somewhere. I don't think they understood exactly what an officer did. Again, it was just a field that was very different from what they had known and wanted for me.

What I do know is that I grew up in the Navy. I matured in Newport. Life had been a bowl of cherries at Yale, and if it had been up to me, I would have still been on campus, taking one cherry at a time as long as I possibly could.

One major life lesson that I learned in Newport was never to play poker. I was horrible at it. Poker was the number one choice of enlisted men to pass the time. My roommate, a fellow who came from some college out West, was particularly good. He pulled me aside after a game and said he felt bad that he made out like a bandit every time I played

"Ted," he said. "Do NOT play poker. When you draw a good hand your face looks as if you hit the gold rush. When you get a bad hand, it's obvious."

I had been wondering why I kept losing when everyone else won. Apparently, I couldn't contain my joy very well. I listened to his advice.

At the end of my time at Newport, I had one chance—about three minutes—to convince my superiors to send me into naval intelligence. Officers interviewed each of us before giving commissions, and what they mainly wanted to know was our preference for ship size and location. To get what I wanted, I would have to channel my inner Hampton Robb.

"Large combatant, small combatant, East Coast, West Coast?" an officer asked at my interview.

I said intelligence.

He laughed. "Officer Candidate Seaman Apprentice Robb, you're headed for ship duty. Now the question is, 'Large combatant, small combatant, East Coast, West Coast?'"

For three minutes I launched into my travel resumé, emphasizing that I would best serve the Navy in intelligence. Others knew how ships worked and how to lead men. I could do that, I said, but I could better serve the military with what I knew about other places.

He said, "Interesting."

I didn't know what would happen.

That officer must have said something to someone, because the day before my June graduation, I received orders to go to the Fleet Intelligence Center, the Navy's first such intelligence station, at Port Lyautey, Morocco. Peg and I would leave soon after our wedding on July 20 and spend a few weeks in Washington, DC, where I would attend intelligence school. I was thrilled—excited to not only secure my dream military post but also move to North Africa. That's how far away I wanted Peg from Mother in Manhattan.

⁖ 38 ⁖

Peg seemed to look forward to our first home on a military base in North Africa as an adventure. She hadn't traveled much at all. I don't think she had ever had a vacation either.

In a way, Peg was raised by two priests. These men had more of an influence on her than any other adult. Largely because of her parents' early deaths, Peg had become quite a devout Catholic, turning to the church consistently for direction and comfort since her early adolescence. When it came time to ask someone for Peg's hand in marriage, I knew whose approval I needed—Father Jim's. Father Jim had known Peg's extended family situation quite well. But his primary concern was for her entrance into the Ryan family. She had two brothers who had run afoul of the law, but I was the one whose family's scandals had fueled New York's gossip magazines.

"You know, your family is not…," he said to me with hesitation, "well…marriage in your family has been more of a convenience than anything else."

I was taken aback. I had never thought of my family history in the way that he did. But how could he have seen it in any other way?

Our patriarch, Thomas Fortune Ryan, had made waves when he married immediately after Ida Barry's death, famously alienating his son, my grandfather Allan. Then a few years later, when Allan decided to marry Irene, he sent

Granny Ryan and all six children packing for Europe where they would live for a year while he set up a new household. And then there was my own mother, who was on her fourth husband. (Uncle Barry, I think, holds the family record with five marriages. His fifth wife was not only his daughter's college roommate, sources say, but also his son's girlfriend at one time). These were only four individuals in a family that held many, many more marital episodes.

Father Jim said he saw no sense of contrition in members of the Ryan family over the years. To him, they were Catholics in name only. He didn't want me to marry Peg and in two years find someone else and get a divorce.

There was nothing I could say in response. He was dead right. My family did have a propensity for being "blasé" about commitments. Feeling jarred, I told him as best I could that marriage was the most important commitment one could make. I feel that very strongly to this day. He must have believed me because I received Father Jim's blessing. Peg and I then talked at length about his concern. She didn't seem bothered.

It's interesting that today, much of the Ryan family history that I have is due to Peg. She researched the family and painstakingly filled in genealogical charts that go back multiple generations. Peg found that, contrary to popular belief, the Ryans had more British roots than Irish. She also clarified Thomas Fortune Ryan's upbringing. Newspapers had printed conflicting stories of his arrival in America. Some stories said his parents had sent him to America as a teenager and others stated that relatives relocated him here when his parents died in Ireland. Peg found that he was born in Virginia to immigrant parents. Nobody else in the Ryan family (that I know of) did such research. I think that for many people who marry multiple times, family history becomes unimportant. Successive partners become less and less interested about those who entered the family before them.

Peg's entrance into the Ryan family was somewhat dramatic. Mother made her displeasure of our engagement known to her brothers and friends, but Peg held her head high and refused to engage in any scenes. I became caught in the middle of a very delicate balancing act. Bob Ellinger took Mother's side while in her presence, but interestingly enough, he kept his opinions to himself otherwise. (And Bob rarely kept his opinions to himself.)

The biggest fracas that broke out was when Peg insisted on paying for the wedding. Mother had hoped that she could control the wedding by controlling its finances, and Peg said no way. It was as if she were standing in the middle of Fifth Avenue with her hands on her hips, yelling, "This is me! By hook or by crook I'm going to get this thing financed!" And, of course, she did. Mother was stunned. She couldn't understand why Peggy, who had barely any earthly goods, wanted to pay for this event.

The Ryans, I'm sure, were stunned as well. I think the family thought that once I committed to marrying Peg, Ryan money was going to have to support both of us. Peg's gutsy stance overturned that whole theory. Somehow the priests helped her find a way to finance a ceremony at St. Patrick's Cathedral and a reception at the Waldorf Astoria.

Mother had wanted to invite the world. For one last time, she wanted to parade me around in front of all of her friends. Then Peg gave her a certain number of people she could invite. Mother hit the roof. I remember getting into it with her.

"Peg is coming up with a way to do all of this," I would repeat. "You can't do this to her."

Because of the size of the Ryan family, Mother's guests were largely relatives. From what I can remember, everyone came. It was a joy to welcome Uncle Phil and Aunt Mary from Canada. They had developed a real love for Peg, and she for them.

On the day of our wedding, I felt scared to death. Not because I was taking a wife, but because I dearly hoped Mother would behave. I didn't know what was going to happen. Mother handled herself very well. Two of Peggy's aunts, on the other hand, got into a big argument because of where they were seated in the pews. One didn't like that the other was placed in front of her. Peg handled it beautifully. Just like she had told me on the Eisenhower campaign that I would take the volunteers she sent and like it, she told her aunts that they would sit where she said and like it. I have every reason to believe that Peg thoroughly enjoyed the day.

Looking back over our wedding photos, I see that three people in particular looked radiant—Peg, me, and Mother.

As a wedding present, Peg handed me a check of all the savings she had left: $125. In lieu of a honeymoon, we went directly to Washington, DC, where we spent a few weeks before flying overseas. I'm pretty sure that by the time the plane took off, Peg was pregnant.

⪻ 39 ⪼

During our short time in Washington, I attended intelligence school. I also received a change of assignment. A superior called me into his office and said I would no longer be heading to Port Lyautey, Morocco, the site of America's first international naval intelligence station. Instead, I'd be going to Bahrain.

"Great," I said. "Where do I catch the bus?"

He stared at me. I thought Bahrain was located in the Washington, DC, area.

"Ensign Robb," he said with wide eyes. "I suggest you get yourself a globe."

I soon realized that Bahrain was an island of about 240 square miles in the Persian Gulf.

According to military procedure, naval officers weren't permitted to take dependents to the Persian Gulf unless they had permission from the admiral. In Newport, I had written a strong letter to the proper authorities asking whether Peg could join me when I reported in August. The office approved my request, but because mail traveled by slow freight, I didn't receive its response before the wedding. So I contacted the Washington office and asked if they could send a telegram to the admiral asking why I hadn't received confirmation. As it turns out, they didn't yet know I was coming. My orders also traveled by slow freight.

When the admiral's office received the Washington telegram, it read, "Ensign Robb requested permission to bring dependent to the station."

"Permission granted, but why are you coming?" the telegram asked.

Soon the orders arrived and all was sorted out. Later I learned that the first mention of my name aroused a lot of speculation as to why a man would want to drop his wife off in the Persian Gulf.

⁖ 40 ⁖

Bahrain was a unique place to live. At the time, it was one of several British protectorates in the Middle East (Bahrain became independent in 1971). The US Navy operated on a British base. My job was to participate in intelligence gathering missions. Several Naval Communications Units operated in the Persian Gulf following World War II. From bases like ours in Bahrain, electronic intelligence aircraft conducted operations from various points throughout Europe and the Middle East.

A Muslim land with many beaches holding exotic wildlife, Bahrain held (and still holds) one of the largest oil refineries in the world. Its citizens followed a conservative Arab lifestyle, although a few thousand civilian British individuals and families lived there as well.

After World War II, Bahrain became a target of riots, the result of increasing anti-British sentiment in the Arab world. Rioting focused, in particular, on the Muslim community. I spoke with many locals at the time about their frustration with America. They were down on us because we leaned so heavily in favor of the Jews, and they felt our pro-Israeli stance wasn't fair. The sheik of Bahrain was married to a Jewish woman, and the nationals felt this fueled American anti-Muslim ideology.

This unrest did concern me, especially as Peg had her entire pregnancy there. She and I had to share a house with another ensign until David's birth. This was an awkward situation, especially as I had to report to the ship every day and Peg was alone much of the time.

At one point, tensions increased when Eisenhower sent troops into Lebanon. To protect its service people, the Navy spoke with the sheik of Bahrain, and he provided a guard for naval housing (located separately from the base). Our guard was something else. I didn't have much faith in his security skills. Sometimes I'd come home and find him—always dressed in white—slumped over at his post. At my approach he'd snap up and present his guns. I was always concerned he would fire accidentally or drop them.

Once, as I prepared to leave for a longer mission, I mapped out an exit route for Peg should social tensions blow up in my absence. Bahrain wasn't an easy place to escape. The airport, for example, was sort of on an island by itself at the northern end. It would have been very easy to become cut off from outside help.

I spoke with a friend we had made named Ali. We had hit it off at one of the many parties thrown by Adm. Briggs. Like many men, Ali had multiple wives. Should something happen in my absence, I asked, would he take Peg into his household and keep her undercover as one of his wives? Ali said, "Of course." He was quite well respected among the people, and I couldn't find a safer place for her. Peg liked Ali very much, but thankfully she never had to move in with his harem.

Peg found ways to occupy herself in her ample time alone. She did meet many other military wives but made few close friends in that group. Some of the women didn't have many outside interests and took to the bottle quite heavily.

Liquor was cheap on the island. As it wasn't permitted in Muslim communities, the US and the British Navy had booze sent to the commissary to keep service families happy. I remember I could get a huge bottle of Scotch for as little as one dollar. And my permit allowed me one-hundred dollars' worth of booze every month. Many of the military wives consumed their family's entire allotment.

There was a Catholic church there attended by mainly naval people. I remember its Irish priest very well. The man was hilarious, perhaps intentionally, perhaps not. He hesitated at nothing to keep parishioners focused on his homilies. Once a child was causing a significant distraction by kicking at the pew. The priest stopped his service, looked at the kid's mother, and said, "If you take off her shoe, she'll stop doing that."

Either through that church or another channel, Peg learned about a British Episcopal missionary woman who taught English classes. She reached out to the woman and volunteered to teach English to a weekly class of about a dozen Iranian girls. She hadn't taught before as I remember, but she loved it.

We even hosted Peg and her class on the ship. The girls normally wore Arab dress as did Peg (who donned a burka every day), but on this occasion, all the young ladies arrived on the ship dressed to the tee. They had a ball. The occasion was an ice cream-making event, as we could make it on board. Peg loved ice cream. As a fellow officer approached our group, he pulled me aside and asked, "Which one is your wife?" Peg was devouring ice cream like a thirteen-year-old and he couldn't tell her apart from her girls.

Her class adored her. They thought Peg was the cat's meow. She kept in touch with them after we returned stateside, and at one point, they invited Peg back to visit, and she went on her own.

WE BOTH LOVED FREQUENTING THE SOUK—A MARKET where you had to haggle with sellers. A vendor might say a bunch of radishes cost the equivalent of ten dollars. We would say, "That's too high." He would say, "Well, what can you spend?" I loved the process and became pretty good at it. I never took anybody's first price for anything.

Early on I had learned not to go to banks to cash my paycheck. The best exchange rate came from local money traders. Because bargaining was so inherent in the economic system, it was possible to negotiate a much better exchange rate this way. I found a wonderful trader. Fun and well-educated, he spoke and understood English. Both of us enjoyed our frequent meetings.

I would lay my check on the table and he'd look at it. He would do some computations and say something like, "I'll give you twenty-five rupees to the dollar."

"No, not good."

He'd tell me why the exchange factor had gone down. And back and forth we would go for about an hour every visit. I could tell when it was time to settle because his voice would change. He would transition suddenly from speaking fluent English to struggling to find the right words to argue my latest objection. That's when I knew I had gone as far as I could and settled. I realized that this was his way of ending the negotiation without insult.

At some point during my deployment, Mother decided she wanted to visit us with Bob Ellinger to assess our situation. I was shocked. But they came, and their trip went well. It was so hot—none of us had ever experienced heat like that. We had only one room with air conditioning in our apartment, so we huddled together in it. And Peg and I had a hoot walking around with them at the souk. They bought all kinds of things. Bob loved bargaining, and he especially enjoyed interacting with the money trader. So did the other officers aboard the ship. I had told them they would get a better exchange rate from this guy than anyone else and, finally, all of the officers started using his services.

I made a special effort to say good-bye to this man before I left.

"Ensign Robb," he said, "I really appreciate your sending me these officers, but they're no fun. They took my first offer every time."

I guess I could pull a pretty good poker face when I needed to after all.

❖ 41 ❖

Every few months a new flagship (a seaplane tender) would come into port with different Middle East officers and crew. Sometimes I would accompany the admiral aboard, and we would go to various places along the Red Sea that you hear about in the news today. At different stops, the senior sheiks would come aboard, share a meal prepared by naval cooks, then invite our top brass ashore for local fare. This was a hard sell, as naval men (during my stay) didn't have an appetite for the locally prepared food. As I was the most junior officer aboard, the senior officers often would delegate me to represent them as a guest. I didn't mind at all.

With about three others from our ship, I would accept the dinner invitation and arrive at whatever home or mosque was hosting it. There I would sit with the sheiks and their officers in front of a goat roasting on a spit. On a table in front of us would sit three bowls of different rice and sauce combinations, and we would rip the goat off the spit, mix it with the rice and sauces and eat it. This was termed a "goat grab" by the Navy, and I got pretty good at it. In fact, I earned the title of "Chief Goat Grabber." I always enjoyed goat grabs—until the next day when everything just ran right out of my backside.

On one such flagship trip, a radioman contacted me and said, "Ensign Robb, you're a father." I was flabbergasted.

Bahrain is located just off Saudi Arabia, and the plan was for Peg to give birth at the Air Force Hospital there. The

Navy had one to two flights going between Bahrain and the mainland every day, so when Peg started having contractions, they flew her over as soon as they could. David was born at the air base in Dhahran. The doctors and nurses were American, and Peg loved them. What she didn't love was being on the front of the tour given to any officials who happened to be visiting the base. A few admirals and generals walked right into her room, and she hated that parade. She was there for about a week of that.

I had hoped that David would be a dual citizen, but US bases are considered US territories, and my aspiration to be the father of a Saudi citizen was not realized.

❖ 42 ❖

We lived in Bahrain for a little over a year. Sometime before we left, my new orders came. I was to go to Norfolk, Virginia, and work in submarine intelligence where I would survey American waters for foreign submarines. The assignment sounded god-awful.

"What a waste!" I muttered. By then, I had come to know the Middle East quite well. So I went to Adm. Briggs.

"I don't feel that the Navy is going to get the best of my talents and ability if they send me to survey submarine activity." I asked if he could help me find a way to better use my knowledge and travel experience.

Once again, I was able to change what I initially was scheduled to do. Hampton would have been proud. Adm. Briggs sent a note to Washington saying I would much better serve the Navy if I worked in Middle East intelligence rather than go to Norfolk. Soon I received new orders. In Washington, DC, I would run the Middle East desk at the Office of Naval Intelligence. It was the perfect assignment for me.

Peg and I moved to Alexandria, Virginia, where with Mother's help we bought our first house. We needed the extra room. Felicia was soon born, making ours a family of four.

⁖ 43 ⁖

President Dwight Eisenhower's second term came to an end while we were back in Washington. Peg and I hadn't been huge fans of Vice President Richard Nixon, but we supported him like good Republican Party stalwarts. Momentum, of course, belonged to Democrat John F. Kennedy.

At the time, I drove a Ford Edsel, a model only on the marketplace for two years because it was such an over-priced lemon of a car. Edsels have gone down in history as one of the worst cars ever made and as an enduring embarrassment for the Ford auto company. My attachment to Edsels will live on in *The Washington Post* archives. One day the paper showcased a picture of me with a caption that I'll never forget.

"The description of the biggest failure in the world is a Yale man in Washington driving an Edsel with a Nixon bumper sticker."

I sent copies to everyone I could think of.

THE HIGHLIGHT OF MY JOB IN DC WAS PARTICIPATING in weekly 7 a.m. briefings where I would give an oral report to Adm. Arleigh Burke, a five-star admiral and chief of naval operations. Burke later was recognized as an essential member of a top-secret team that spearheaded a submarine-launched ballistic missiles program. Military scholars have credited Burke's efforts as equipping America with the nuclear defense front it needed to deter nuclear attacks during the Cold War. Before the admiral's tenure, the Navy had played second fiddle to the Army in military strategy; the submarine program gave the branch more of a presence at the joint chiefs' table.

I would always start my presentation with a complete picture of where we had naval members present in Middle East waters. Burke, to my knowledge, hadn't ever spent much time in that part of the world. His command during World War II had taken place in the South Pacific. Nevertheless, the admiral had a comprehensive knowledge of all international affairs. I found his questions detailed and challenging to answer.

At one point, Burke's chief of staff questioned a report I made about the disposition and number of US ships in one area. He said my numbers and location were wrong.

With respect, I disagreed. I said I had double-checked my information before the meeting and was positive.

"Lt. Robb," Adm. Burke said, "I'm so sure that we're right that I will buy you a Scotch and water if we're wrong."

Burke was a great man. His chief of staff was not. That captain was very sensitive to protocol, and on this occasion, he was furious with me. He thought I, a junior grade lieutenant, had no business correcting him.

So, of course, I rushed back to the office and checked the data to find that I was indeed correct.

At the next briefing, Adm. Burke came in and started by saying he had been wrong.

"It appears I have lost a bet," he said.

Suddenly a staff member carrying a scotch and soda on a tray walked up to me. It was only 7:30 a.m. But you bet I drank it.

I LOVED THE NAVY, BUT I KNEW I COULDN'T MAKE A career of it. At the time, the Navy favored promotions for officers who had graduated from the Naval Academy. No matter how hard you worked, if you hadn't gone to school there, you were treated like a lesser naval officer. To people like the admiral's chief of staff, I was a "90-day Newport wonder" who would never be an equal because he hadn't shared in the history of the Naval Academy. Had promotion been an option, I would have stayed. I even had the opportunity to take a class in Russian at the intelligence school. I had learned a little bit on the trip with Charlie Lord and had returned home from Europe in awe of people who could speak multiple languages. I would have enjoyed picking up as many as I could and continuing a career in military intelligence. But when the DC term came to an end, I had a family of four to provide for. I knew I needed more than what the military would offer me.

Just before I left, I had another run-in with that chief of staff regarding observations I had made at one of the weekly briefings. There had been threats of a military coup in Turkey, but I assured the admiral that we had nothing to worry about. By noon that same day, I was proven dead wrong. The coup had indeed occurred. The first person who called me was this captain.

"I want to let you know there was a coup in Turkey. Do you have anything to say?"

"Yes, I'm retiring next week," I answered.

"Yale smart ass," he grumbled.

⁖ 44 ⁖

What I wanted to do most was return to the Middle East with some type of international role. Before my military service ended, I knocked on the doors of several companies asking how I might find such a position in their ranks. In every case, I was told that I would have to put in a year or two of grunt work selling widgets or whatever, then gradually earn entrance into an international office.

One such company told me about an alternative. There was an international business school in Arizona. After a year of coursework there at the American Institute for Foreign Trade, I would be eligible for jobs that companies would present on that very campus. I decided we would move to Arizona.

By that time, Bob Ellinger had started asking me about my future plans.

"What are you going to do next?"

I told him about my plan to go into international business by way of this Arizona program. I felt confident that I would find employment at the end of a year there.

Mother and Bob thought this was ridiculous. Neither of them put much stock in extra schooling. I don't know why they cared so much.

Bob in particular was dead set on my becoming a stockbroker. He insisted that I take an interview that he secured for me at a Wall Street firm. I went but purposely stunk up the whole thing. I rambled on ad nauseum, making sure that I gave ridiculous answers to whatever was asked. At one point, I went on a tangent about why I thought corporations should not have assets or investments in South Africa. It was something I had read in the newspapers, but I knew little about the topic.

Finally, the guy said, "Nice to have met you, Ted."

By the time I arrived back at the apartment, Bob had received a phone call.

"Don't press him to become an investment banker," the man said to him. "He's not interested."

Blowing off that interview was such a smart idea. It made Bob finally lay off.

Mother though decided to limit my financial support. She believed I wasn't taking their sound advice and was making a fool of myself. I couldn't have disagreed more.

NEARLY TWO DECADES AFTER MOTHER AND MAL HAD put me alone on a train headed west, I was going back to Arizona. This time, I had company: Peg, David, Felicia, and I headed for Glendale, just north of Phoenix.

⁚ 45 ⁚

Today the American Institute for Foreign Trade is known as the Thunderbird School of Global Management at Arizona State University. When I arrived in 1961, it had been operating as an independent institution for over a decade, begun at the request of Army Air Training Command in an effort to train veterans for international business opportunities.

Of the approximately 200 people in my class, a good number had never served in the military. All that was required for admittance, I believe, was a college degree or a high school diploma and two years of work experience. By eastern standards, the curriculum was not at all challenging. The program resembled a type of today's learning courses in that it was modular-led by visiting professors. Most teachers were retired business professionals who mainly shared their international experiences. Some of their "sea stories" were fascinating, but I had hoped the program might offer an in-depth study of topics like international economics, trade, and tariff policies. Nevertheless, companies that didn't want to vet candidates themselves flocked to schools like this to bolster their international staff. Enrollment alone gave me the qualification companies wanted—a presence on a "foreign trade" campus. Ironically, the best business lessons I learned in Arizona happened off campus.

THE MODULAR SCHEDULE WAS SO LOOSEY-GOOSEY THAT
it made finding work off campus difficult. Without my
mother's help, I had to do something to provide for the
family. One day between course blocks, I saw an advertisement for Fuller Brush salespeople in the newspaper. I
realized this type of work would offer me a flexible schedule, and depending on how much time I could dedicate,
provide me enough income to survive.

When I tell associates now that I once worked as a Fuller
Brush man, they guffaw—particularly those who know my
family's history.

"The great-grandson of Thomas Fortune Ryan, a Fuller
Brush man?!"

I can see where people might find it a rather humbling
position—going door to door with a catalog, seeing what
housewives might want to buy, and having doors slammed
in my face. But I never thought of it that way. I saw the
opportunity, needed a job, and took it. At the time, salespeople earned a good percentage of sales.

I remember my first day on the job. The thought of ring-
ing a stranger's doorbell cold scared me to death. The ad had
said that the company would provide training, so I thought,
"This is good. I'll shadow someone for a while and learn the
best ways to craft my sales pitch." Well, my "mentor" had a
different type of introduction in mind. We met and he took
me to a neighborhood within his sales territory. I followed
him up to one house and watched him make a sale. Then
we went back to his car and he said, "Now you see, that's
how it's done." He pointed down the street. "Go down there
and back, and I'll be back in an hour." That was my training.

I had flipped through the catalog but had little idea
what I was selling. One woman said she would buy some

refrigerator deodorant. I said we didn't have any. She took the catalog, showed me the page where it was featured, and said, "Yes, you do." So I made a few sales that first day.

I was hard on myself at first. If I rang a bell and nobody answered, or slammed the door in my face, I took it as a personal insult. It took me awhile to realize that some people just didn't want to buy anything. Dad was clearly in the back of my mind with every door that I approached. Perhaps it was him who I would hear saying, "You can make this sale. You have to work on it. Don't run away."

One location gave me fair warning of a difficult sales visit. I walked up to a house that had signs all over the yard saying things like "No peddlers, agents, and/or solicitors…" But I knocked anyway.

A lovely woman opened the door and invited me inside. Everything I said fascinated her. She wanted so many things that I thought I had hit a gold mine. Writing down the codes for all of the items she chose, I was on the second or third page of an order when I heard a deep voice.

"Can't you read?"

I turned around and saw the biggest truck driver I have ever seen in my life. The size and attitude of this man just stunned me, especially as the woman was young and quite dainty with religious icons around her home.

"Yes," I stammered.

"Not very well."

He forced me up by the scruff of my neck and threw me out of the house as his wife begged him to be nice. My sales kit followed behind me. Apparently, his wife must have been the star customer for every business north of Phoenix.

I relished that job. And when my class schedule kept me from keeping up with my route, Peg stepped in. She was great—and also pregnant with Greg, our third child. Peg was so good at sales that she and I would compete to see who had the better record. The customers loved her, but, boy, did I hear it from some women customers who couldn't believe I had my pregnant wife doing my job.

The most valuable assignment I had at the American Institute for Foreign Trade led me to research a paper encouraging Fuller Brush to open an international division. It was a great opportunity to connect my studies with my sales experience. I sent it to the company but never heard anything. About eight years later, I read in the paper that the company had opened a British division. I entertained wonderfully wild dreams that I had put a bug in somebody's ear.

So many times in my young life, I can see now, I made choices that sidestepped my pride. These choices led to experiences that anchored me. For example, had I not immersed myself in stable duties, I never would have benefited so much from a connection to a horse. Had I not asked for different-minded Yale roommates who lived west of the Hudson River, I would have limited my personal growth. Had I not engaged as many locals as possible in Eastern Europe, I would have been only a tourist, not a student of other cultures. Had I not been willing to ask the feisty, beautiful woman from the Lower East Side to lunch, knowing full well she might respond with a "no," I never would have fallen in love and married Peg.

And had I not answered a newspaper ad and found a job going door to door around Glendale, Arizona, opening myself up to scorn and rejection, I wouldn't have entered a position that taught me how to read people, understand what they wanted, and make a sale. It was the perfect preparation for someone interested in politics.

As I had hoped, when my year at the American Institute for Foreign Trade came to a close, I was offered a job (actually two jobs) through interviews held on campus. I accepted work at Heinz, which had offices in Europe, Latin America, Asia, and Australia. My role would be assistant to the vice president of the international division.

One week after Greg was born, we headed to Pittsburgh in a car that held an infant and two toddlers in the backseat. That was one of the wilder drives I've ever been on. Peg was a great believer in visiting friends when we could, so we stopped along the way to do just that. On one side trip, we met with her younger brother and his family in Kansas. These reprieves on the road kept our hair-raising trip manageable. That was important.

Once in Pittsburgh, we would engage in a far greater challenge than any other I would experience in my life.

⁘ 46 ⁘

A s soon as we arrived in Pittsburgh, Peg became unusually quiet. She had hoped that my career would take us back to New York City. I had told her that Pittsburgh was a huge step in that direction, but neither the thought nor the reality of western Pennsylvania turned her on.

She drew further and further inside herself. I couldn't understand why. At first I assumed it was the pressure of moving, combined with our exhausting cross-country trip and the demands of three kids under four years old. When Peg had gone into the Phoenix hospital with Greg, we hadn't had a babysitter of any kind. I took a week off from Thunderbird to stay at home with David and Felicia and realized just how many things you have to do for little ones. I knew that Peg would have her hands full with these responsibilities and those of an infant, but I hadn't considered what kind of toll that might take on her.

I tried talking to her but couldn't draw more than a "yes" or a "no." I asked if I had done something to upset her. She wouldn't answer. I started getting really worried. I didn't know who to talk to, certainly not Mother or Bob Ellinger. Mother was still in the process of asking herself, "Why the hell did he marry this poverty-stricken woman?" and Bob seemed to only focus on money. I couldn't talk to friends because this was something that happened within the family. I didn't want to share my concerns with anyone. I wanted to protect Peg but didn't know how. It was doubly hard to hack a job at Heinz—for which I would need to travel abroad for up to a month at a time—because I was so worried about leaving her and the kids at home.

Today I recognize this period as the hardest of my life.

"What have I done?" I asked myself again and again. I blamed myself for getting her pregnant so quickly and often. This woman had been a professional secretary into her midtwenties. She had a thriving career and work that satisfied her. Then we got married and she was pregnant almost every day of our time together. I was mystified. I didn't know how we would make it through this. I called on my guardian angel to help me, but I knew it was Peg's angel that needed to pull through.

Peg had kept in touch with Father Jim, one of the priests who had helped raise her. I had always respected Father Jim, his forthrightness with me, and his fondness for Peg. We spoke on the phone and he offered to visit. This gave us a lifeline. His presence helped to cheer up Peg, and she was willing to listen to his sound counsel. From the moment I had called, he suspected that Peg might be suffering from postpartum depression. It turns out that is exactly what she had. I had never heard of this condition before. Even if I had, I don't know that I would have considered it because Peg always wanted lots of children and she thrived during each pregnancy.

Father Jim advised Peg to go to the doctor and see a specialist. He had contacts in Pittsburgh and knew or learned of a psychiatrist with Catholic interests. Peg and I both were the type that wouldn't take an aspirin if we had splitting headaches (for fear of becoming addicted to painkillers). But thank God that Father Jim came. Peg never would have gone to the doctor if not for his encouragement.

Father Jim knew that we would need more than medical help. He asked if I had spoken to my mother about the situation. I said, "No way." She suspected something was wrong, I think, but I would never divulge Peg's condition to her. At one point, I remember Bob Ellinger saying something like, "This wouldn't have happened if you hadn't married someone like Peg."

Father Jim asked if he could meet with Mother and talk to her. I said okay. I'm not sure what exactly he said, but Mother called soon afterward. She asked if she could underwrite the cost of a housekeeper. That's when I hired Lorena, an African American woman who became a beloved member of the house.

The doctor, meanwhile, educated Peg and me about postpartum depression. I was relieved to hear that it wasn't all my fault. (Catholics love guilt. We wallow in it.) The doctor told Peg that he thought she had a very serious case, and he recommended shock treatment. Even at the time, it was a controversial option. But both she and I didn't know what else to do except follow his advice, especially at the urging of Father Jim. The doctor accompanied her to a mental hospital, where she had the treatment over three days. Lorena stayed at home to take care of the children.

At the end of those three days, I remember picking Peg up. I could tell it had been a royally rough treatment. The doctor said he was satisfied enough that he didn't think she needed another bout of it. She looked so wrung out that I didn't want her to have any more. I prayed mightily that Peg would be able to move through this period. And she did—slowly. Later she told me about the treatment. What I heard sent shivers down my spine.

Lorena's presence was a wonderful addition to the household. She took a lot of pressure off of Peg's shoulders, especially after the shock treatment. Father Jim stayed in close touch with us and continued to offer advice as we asked. I'm so pleased that he did because Peg was very frustrated with the doctor when he told her she shouldn't give birth to any more children. She had envisioned having a houseful.

"You're putting yourself at risk," I told her.

Father Jim agreed with the doctor. This was a godsend. The next challenge to consider was how we could cohabit without her becoming pregnant again. I thought we would use prophylactics, but she said no because the Catholic Church didn't condone them. She said we would use the rhythm method.

"I'm no mathematician," I said. "I can't count the days. I need something I can visually look at."

So on the days when she was least likely to get pregnant, Peg would put a small flower behind her ear. That was a lovely signal for me. Otherwise, I was petrified to touch her.

It's very hard to talk about this episode in our lives now. I can only hope that it will help someone else to read what we went through. As best as I can say, I think that horrible shock treatment worked. Something happened during those three days in the hospital to improve her mental health. For the rest of our years together, I watched to see if she was showing signs of slipping into that darkness. I didn't notice them again after those early Pittsburgh days.

❖ 47 ❖

As Peg felt stronger, I decided it would be a good idea to move away from the house associated with such dark memories. We bought a home outside Pittsburgh in Fox Chapel, and I think it helped give her a new lease on life. A little less than a year or so after I joined the Heinz team, we were both ready to start socializing again. If I'm honest, I'll say one of my main motivations was to help Peg find a social network that would keep her calendar full of things to focus on outside of the house.

When we had moved to Alexandria, I had contacted the Yale alumni office for a list of classmates who lived in the area, and I did the same in Pittsburgh. Yale put me in touch with a college friend named Ned Ruffin. He was eager to get our families together and wanted Peg to meet his wife, who went by the nickname "Punkin." I had no idea what sort of woman would go by that name. Sometimes these social influencers can be insufferable, surrounded by an air of "I'm the one who makes things run around here." But Punkin was just a gem and the contact of all contacts to have in the Pittsburgh area. With a wonderful laugh and full of natural warmth, she invited us over and introduced us to everybody she knew.

That first interaction became the start of several wonderful years. I wasn't thrilled with the Heinz job. I had it for about four years, and although I loved the travel— sometimes visiting England, Italy, and Australia for up to a month—I became absent at home. I noticed one afternoon that the kids were happier to meet the mailman than they had been to greet me on my most recent return home. That knocked me out. I realized a gap was widening between me and my family. I felt like a fifth wheel. Something told me that if I stayed in my current position, I'd get a divorce and lose Peg and the kids. I told Peg that I thought I needed to try changing positions at Heinz. She hadn't said anything about it, but as soon as I introduced the topic, the floodgates opened and she heartily agreed.

Heinz started training me for a domestic marketing position. This new post gave me a chance to engage with the family in what became a golden social period. We have a photo album full of pictures from this time. Each snapshot looks like a Kodachrome family movie moment—lots of smiles, freckled sunburns, adults holding cocktails and shaking with laughter. In and around Fox Chapel we constantly went on outings, trekking to picnics and swimming pools in the summers, ice skating ponds and sledding hills in the winters, and parties all year-round. An annual highlight was the "Town and Gown" outdoor event hosted by the women. It featured a softball game for all the adults: the men would bat left-handed so the women could compete. And did they ever. Once Peg hit a home run and the kids were stunned.

The album also contains photos of the visitors we entertained. Part of my job involved entertaining international businessmen and their families who would come to Pittsburgh to learn about Heinz before taking or expanding operations abroad. I remember a Japanese man, a fellow Heinz executive, who came and spent months with us. He loved skiing, and we took him up to Mont Tremblant in

Quebec, a resort started by Joseph Ryan, one of my grandfather Allan's brothers.

We also have several pictures taken with the Luscombe family. At the time, Kevin Luscombe was my Australian counterpart. We spent many, many days entertaining him and his family of seven. Kevin had the most wonderful dry wit. Peg and I both loved him. He later visited us a couple of times in Philadelphia, and we saw his family in Australia. Kevin became such a marketing force during and after his time at Heinz that newspapers there have called him "the godfather of Australian marketing."

Early on, Punkin Ruffin's wonderful social gatherings reunited me with another Yale friend, Jack McGregor. It was Jack who started me on a political trajectory that would redirect my professional interests.

Miriam Ryan Robb and Theodore Robb, 1937.

Hampton Robb gives away his daughter Roberta, circa 1950.

Ted Robb, 1944

Arizona Day School (Ted seated in first row on far left), 1945.

Robert "Bob" Ellinger and Miriam Ryan Robb Ellinger, 1947.

Ted and his childhood governess Malvine "Mal" DeConinck, 1949.

Margaret "Peggy" Armstrong marries Theodore Ryan Robb, 1957.

Ensign Robb at Officer Candidate School, 1957.

Robb family at Ted's swearing in ceremony as Regional Administrator of HUD, 1971.

Ted and Peg Robb at niece Roxanne Armstrong's wedding, 1992.

Robb family celebrating Ted's honorary doctorate from Lincoln University (Front L-R: Jeffrey, Greg, Joanne Hurt, Eleanor "Ellie," Ted, Felicia Robb Vargas, Alec Paterson, David, Joan Paterson. Back L-R: Peg, Joel Vargas, Elizabeth Robb), 2006.

Pomfret High School 50th Class Reunion (L-R: David Lyon, Kate Robinson, Gilbert "Gil" Chapman, Charles "Chuck" Henry), 2002.

Ted with grandchildren Caroline and Hunter Robb, circa 2014.

Ted's 87th birthday celebration (Front L-R: Felicia, Elizabeth, Ted, Caroline. Back L-R: Joel, Jeffrey, Greg, Hunter, David, nephew Christian Armstrong, Ellie), 2021.

ACT TWO

⁓

"I have always held that if he who bases his hopes on human nature is a fool, he who gives up in the face of circumstances is a coward."

—ALBERT CAMUS

⸵ 48 ⸵

It might have been at a cocktail party that Jack McGregor asked if I would help him run for state Senate. He knew of my political history—that Peg and I worked for Youth for Eisenhower, that Uncle Ted was a Connecticut state senator, and that my family had significant party leanings. Seeking office in Pittsburgh was an uphill battle for any Republican at the time. Allegheny County had been run by Democrats for as long as most people could remember. But McGregor, a lawyer and father of four, was up for the challenge. He didn't have much money to start a campaign, so the effort would require a lot of creative thinking. Especially because most of Pittsburgh had no idea who he was.

My first step was to find some seed money. I approached the people we called the "Republican fat cats" in Pittsburgh. They had money, and we needed it. Their response angers me to this day.

"We don't put money down a rathole," they said.

I volunteered to serve as treasurer of Jack's campaign. The last thing I wanted was for him to go into debt. Jack wasn't risk-averse. Soon after his run, he would start another campaign, one to bring a National Hockey League franchise to Pittsburgh after the last one left during the Depression. He was successful, becoming the founder and first owner of the Pittsburgh Penguins. Two years later, after also investing in a professional soccer team, he realized he was overextended and had to sell the Penguins.

I told Jack that if I sensed the campaign was going to hit his personal finances, I would cancel certain events on the itinerary.

"If the outflow is too high," I said, "I'll try to prevent certain expenditures."

To his credit, he agreed. Success in politics without money is a near impossibility. But I had faith in the skills I had developed during my Fuller Brush days. I decided we would get the word out about Jack and raise funds by going door to door in targeted neighborhoods. I knew I needed something catchy to get his name stuck in people's minds so that voters just might elect the first Republican they had in years. I drew inspiration from my time working the horse racing circuit with Uncle Barry.

In horse racing, gamblers with pari-mutuel tickets play the odds to win bets on a winning horse. We had tickets made up with McGregor's name on them, and we "sold" each one for two dollars. It was a way of connecting a candidate to voters in a way they could get excited about.

"Put two dollars on McGregor to win!" the ticket read.

It worked like a charm. People contributed to our campaign and received their ticket while learning about McGregor's goals. Reports came back on election night that as people voted, they gripped their tickets as if they were wagering on a horse.

Soon after we won, a check for $15,000 arrived in the mail from the same wealthy Republicans who had turned us down at the start. Jack told me I could handle our response.

I returned the check along with a post-it that read, "Some rathole."

᠅ 49 ᠅

I n 1964, Governor William Scranton initiated the Pennsylvania Human Relations Commission to investigate racial injustice throughout the state. Jack contacted me and said Scranton wanted me on the committee. At first, I thought it was my prowess until I realized that Scranton wanted a diverse, bipartisan commission, and I fit the social demographic of the suburban, white Catholic that he needed. Nevertheless, my participation on this commission was a turning point.

The commission met quarterly to review complaints raised by whistleblowers at institutions that received state funds. After the executive director of the commission staked out the situations, he would refer them to us and we would vote on which ones we believed warranted our action. Then we would function as a jury of sorts.

I had read of government infighting at the expense of civil rights in the newspapers, but cases that came before the commission opened my eyes to malfeasance that I hadn't realized existed. Before my tenure, Scranton had started the commission to investigate the lack of desegregation in the Chester County school system. It found that school authorities were guilty as hell, too scared of bullish white parents to adhere to federal directives on mixed-race education. During my year on the commission, I also remember hearing elder abuse cases. I had no idea this topic existed. More than a few times we considered situations of child and elder abuse, and I came to realize that it is at the two ends of our lives that we are physically weakest and thus more apt to be abused. During on-site visits, I noted that nursing homes more often than not are directed by institutions rather than individuals. Something about this repelled me. I didn't know it at the time, but one day I would work to further a different model of elder care.

It was these meetings that first gave me exposure to Philadelphia—and to the types of bipartisan engagement that could bring productive changes to government. I remember participating in lively discussions with Harry Boyer, a Democrat and the head of the AFL/CIO union. Our ability to push and learn from each other would bring me good fortune a few years later, and our efforts to negotiate settlements provided good training for my future challenges.

⸭ 50 ⸭

When I joined the domestic marketing team at Heinz, I came into closer contact with future senator John Heinz IV, the great-grandson of the company's founder. He joined the company after graduating from Yale four years after me. I liked Johnny very much. Other than with him and one other, I didn't associate much with my co-workers. I found the Heinz company very conservative. Corporate decisions were labored, and the overall vision was stuck in the past. Heinz seemed happy to drift along thinking it would forever be the ketchup, baby food, and soup producer of the world. Only the international division seemed innovative in any way.

Salaries also were not competitive. At Christmastime, instead of a bonus, they gave us a Heinz trinket. One year, we received a coin with the founder's picture imprinted on it. I remember walking down to the Allegheny River with a co-worker and skipping the coin like a rock into the river.

Johnny Heinz, though, brought a breath of fresh air with him. He gave and sponsored me for opportunities that I never would have qualified for otherwise.

I had received some local recognition for my association with Jack McGregor's campaign, and Johnny was a notable Republican donor. Johnny nurtured my political interests by encouraging me to work for the party while on the company's pay. For two weeks in 1964, the Heinz company essentially cut me loose to campaign for Pennsylvania Governor Scranton at the Republican National Convention in San Francisco.

In the six months leading up to the convention, Scranton had become a front-runner to take the Republican nomination from Barry Goldwater, a senator from Arizona. President Lyndon Johnson would be the Democratic candidate in the election later that year. As vice president, Johnson had been sworn in as president on November 22, 1963, after President John F. Kennedy was assassinated.

I think I was in my first year at Heinz when my secretary told me that Kennedy had been assassinated. She knew of my Republican bias, and I remember saying to her something like, "Are you just trying to pull my chain?" I thought she was kidding. I certainly had never witnessed anything like the press coverage that followed, particularly its investigations into Lee Harvey Oswald. The focus on Oswald took attention away from foreign involvement, but it did mention that he had contacts with at least one Russian entity. I highly suspected Russian engagement. My trip to Russia and Ambassador Bohlen's conversations deeply resonated with this theory. I kept thinking of the ambassador pointing out that bug behind the American seal. In my mind, somebody had planted a seed in Oswald's mind. I remember talking about this with Charlie Lord and he thought the same thing. Although I was no Kennedy fan at the time, in hindsight I've had much more appreciation for him, his stance on the Bay of Pigs, and seemingly fearless standoff with Russia.

As Johnson took office in 1963, liberal and moderate Republicans began backing New York Governor Nelson Rockefeller as the front-runner to the 1964 Republican nomination. But Rockefeller's campaign lost a lot of steam in the months leading up to the convention. Never an aggressive candidate, Rockefeller didn't have a good strategy for overcoming Goldwater's assertion that he was a symbol of eastern liberals. He also couldn't get past the disapproval of social conservatives when he married a woman within a year of divorcing his first wife. Should Rockefeller have emerged as the candidate, Scranton could very well have become his vice presidential pick. A lot of people thought Scranton would have been a good vice president, including the governor himself. I don't think Scranton expected momentum to swing his way, but in the summer of 1964 he became the front-runner to challenge Goldwater for the Republican nomination.

Johnny Heinz wanted to employ my talents, but it also was politically smart for the company to travel to the site of the Republican convention in San Francisco to support Scranton. The idea sounded great, but I hardly wanted to leave Peg without consulting her after traveling so much for work. I asked what she thought of the opportunity.

"If you don't go," she responded, "I will."

It was so expensive to call long distance in those days that we agreed I wouldn't phone home unless there was some emergency. To save money, I reached out to Tersh Boasberg, a good friend of mine from Yale who had migrated to San Francisco after finishing Harvard Law School. Tersh, a fierce Democrat, happily said he would put me up on his couch.

WHEN I ARRIVED IN SAN FRANCISCO IN MID-JULY OF 1964, my job was to serve as Scranton's eyes and ears within the New Jersey delegation. Former New Jersey governor Christine Todd Whitman's father was then the state party chairman, and we had great hopes that New Jersey would pull for Scranton.

Both the Scranton and Goldwater campaigns set up headquarters at the sensational Mark Hopkins Hotel, which overlooked the city and the bay from its perch in San Francisco's ritzy Nob Hill neighborhood. On the first day of the convention, I worked on the hotel's twelfth floor with other campaigners. The atmosphere outdoors was electric. The convention slogan—"GOParty 1964"—decorated badges, bumper stickers, jewelry, and signs. San Francisco fully embraced the national spotlight.

As I exited the hotel, I ran smack into a gorgeous young woman wearing nothing above her waist but a button on each nipple. One read "Scranton" and the other "Goldwater." My OCS roommate from Newport would have shaken his head because, once again, my face registered my every emotion. An Associated Press photographer snapped a photo of me ogling this woman along with a group of men who had gathered behind me.

Back home, *The Pittsburgh Post-Gazette* ran the photo, featuring the bare back of the woman, at the head of its second section under the headline "Funny Business at the Republican Convention." Peg's phone rang off the hook with calls from everyone except me. I had no idea about the picture until I came home.

I LOVED THE CLIMATE AND THE PEOPLE OF SAN FRANCISCO. I'd heard that a few of my acquaintances had moved west for jobs there, and I entertained the thought of relocating my family. During the day, delegations would caucus, cheer, and blow whistles, and candidates would meet with them. Political conventions are exhausting for the candidates and a party for the delegates. To my utter enjoyment, Uncle Ted and I crossed paths.

As planned, I worked within the Whitman-led New Jersey delegation. New Jersey ended up as one of the ten states that polled favorably for Scranton. But Goldwater won on the first vote. That night, I tied one on with other campaign workers and woke up with a raging hangover. Wrecked from far too many gin and tonics, I joined the Pennsylvania delegation in the convention hall.

Governor Scranton entered after I did, and all television cameras were on him as he walked down the center aisle to thank his delegation as a graceful loser. For some reason, God bless him, he picked the row where I was sitting. Desperately hungover, I looked particularly devastated. Scranton sat down next to me and draped his arm around my shoulder.

Peg saw the moment, as did many of our Pittsburgh friends, because footage of it hit the news that night. The very same people who had called Peg a couple of days before called her again.

There was short-lived talk of Goldwater asking Scranton to become his vice president; Goldwater's team needed progressive Republicans on board to successfully defeat incumbent President Johnson. Scranton, though, had no interest in serving with Goldwater. I'm not even positive Scranton wanted the presidential nomination. He stepped up, I think, more to help his party defeat a candidate like Goldwater.

I thought Goldwater was a disaster. That nomination was a real blow for many of us. The party just seemed to turn upside-down. People liked Goldwater in the same vein that they later liked Donald Trump and his "Make America Great Again" persona. A senator from Arizona, Goldwater exposed discomfort in parts of the country that hadn't received a lot of attention before. He established himself as a straight talker, and in doing so, separated himself from the political power structure that a lot of westerners didn't trust. Goldwater tapped a vein, but there was a brazen quality to his supporters. I remember watching a delegate spit on the ground as Rockefeller gave a concession speech. It shocked me that someone would disrespect a candidate in that way.

I voted for Johnson in that presidential election, which marked the first time I voted for a Democrat. I wouldn't do so again until Jimmy Carter ran against Ronald Reagan in 1980.

Sometime after Goldwater's defeat, I learned that the American Institute for Foreign Trade was a Goldwater initiative. I also realized that as he aged, Goldwater veered from his more extremist views and started taking a broader position. I had been so dead set against the man and his god-awful campaign that I never thought I would say that he did have some interesting perspectives. I learned that you can't paint somebody all bad because there might be some issues you agree on.

When I returned home from San Francisco, Peg and I had a great laugh together about the newspaper photo and the newsreel. She told me about all of the calls she received, and I was perplexed. I had no idea that I had been featured in either. The folks at Heinz got a good laugh out of that as well. I remember running into Frank Armour, then president of Heinz, who poked fun at my convention role.

"Ted, you did such a good job in California, we're thinking of sending you to Campbell's Soup (our main competitor). We figure you can make them lose."

It was a quip in jest. I laughed.

⁌ 51 ⁌

When Governor Scranton announced that he wouldn't run for reelection, Ray Shafer, his lieutenant governor, started campaigning for the position. By now Johnny Heinz was making a move for a political presence, and he encouraged me to take another leave from Heinz so I could help Shafer. My job was to run "Citizens for Shafer," a grass-roots effort to convince Pittsburgh's working class to vote Republican.

I liked Shafer very much. I had gotten to know him when McGregor ran for state senator, and it made sense that he and Heinz wanted me to serve in this capacity. McGregor had such an upset victory that our whole team had received a lot of interest; I, for one, had received other inquiries to help with campaigns. It was at this point I realized I might have a future in this type of work.

Shafer had different challenges than Scranton had faced. Scranton was a popular governor with a good name and wide-ranging appeal. He didn't need to court the type of voter that Shafer needed. After Goldwater's successful run at the Republican convention, followed by his election loss, the party had to work to realign itself so that Democrats didn't recruit the moderate Republican voter. I remember one Republican donor in particular (a progressive named Elsie Hillman) who worried that Shafer would become swallowed by the feckless Republicans controlling the party in Allegheny County. There was really nobody in control, and we most certainly did not want to associate with only the most conservative players. Citizens for Shafer gave us the ability to reach a new demographic without distancing the old.

I also reached out to well-known Scranton followers and catered to them for contributions. By now I had engaged in a conversation or two with one of the "fat cats" who had referred to McGregor's campaign as a "rathole." He pretty much admitted that the establishment had been wrong not to back Jack and that my post-it was well taken. One of the men in his circle, a member of an old, wealthy Pittsburgh family, made a significant donation that kept our office alive when we were down to our last few dollars.

Citizens for Shafer helped give Ray a foothold in Pittsburgh. But following Scranton was not easy. Shafer was not only less popular but also had to foot the bill for Scranton's insightful initiatives. I thought he managed the job well. Many candidates make promises during their campaigns and then, upon winning, abandon them. Shafer ran on fourteen points that covered a host of items, all of which I thought were compelling, especially two involving workers compensation. As soon as he took office, he told his Cabinet, "I want every one of those fourteen points pursued." And by the time he left office, he could say that he had followed up on each.

Soon after he won, Shafer contacted me. He wanted to create a position for a consultant who could advise nonprofits and other organizations on how to access state funds to pursue job-training opportunities. There were so many layers to accessing grant awards and mobilizing tax dollars that organizations often didn't make use of available funding. Shafer wanted to eliminate the wasted dollars. Seeing me as someone interested in politics, he wanted to reward my work for him and to give me increased experience. Taking the job, though, meant moving the family to Harrisburg.

I went first to Johnny Heinz. He encouraged me to take a two-year leave and have the option to return to the company. I said no to this. I thought it was important to cut the ties and limit any conflict of interest.

In my advisory role, I had carte blanche to learn about sources of government funding within the various state agencies. The only people I really answered to were the governor and one of his Cabinet members, a man named John Tabor who served as secretary of internal affairs. Tabor was a great help and someone who assisted my cutting through lots of red tape.

The first thing I did was obtain a list of people who ran grant programs and met with them to find out how their funding compared to others. Once I got a good handle on that, I identified unnecessary barriers that kept organizations from accessing financial assistance. Certain awarded grants, for example, required reports and estimates that pricey consultants needed to prepare—such costly work distanced many from pursuing payments. On the flip side, I met with nonprofits and helped them troubleshoot the process by developing training programs that aided them in understanding how to use their tax dollars. Most of these groups were closely aligned with the Democratic Party and suspicious of me, a consultant to a Republican governor. Ultimately they were quite pleased that I could help them get their dollars.

Not everyone was happy though. Democrats in the legislature thought Shafer had created a ghost of a job just for me. Herb Fineman, Speaker of the House, referred to my efforts as unnecessary. His exact words in the newspaper called me "an illegal improper excess."

"At least he didn't call me immoral," I said to Peg.

Fineman thought I was getting paid for no substantive work, but that wasn't true. Ray Shafer was quick to back my role as essential to the very groups that supported Fineman. The insult made me feel good. Obviously, I was doing something worth noticing.

I thought to myself, "This is a wonderful way to start my sojourn in the public sector."

⸙ 52 ⸙

I was happy for Peg to take charge of finding a home in Harrisburg. She had been so frustrated with our first home in Pittsburgh, and so longing to return to New York, that we both thought we would end up in downtown Harrisburg, where we knew there was a church we would attend. Once again, Peg shocked me.

On a house-hunting trip, someone had told her about a large guesthouse for rent on a farm in rural Bowmansdale. Peg went to visit and met Dottie Latham, wife of a wealthy lawyer named Ernie Latham. The Lathams lived in a farmhouse and were looking for a family to rent their guesthouse. Peg made a commitment to lease it before I even visited. I remember driving into Harrisburg and her saying, "I've found the most wonderful place." I thought she was talking about one in town, only to be introduced to a laconic farm.

I said, "Peg, how can we end up here when you were so interested in living in the city?"

But she and Dottie had hit it off so well, and Peg could sense that it would be a wonderful place to raise the kids. Her instincts were correct. We lived there for four years. My work in Harrisburg gave me more time to be at home, and I made a real effort to make family dinners every night. In the evenings, we would take long walks around the property and the kids would take turns riding horseback as I led our horse along a creek and through woods. Our social life never bested that in Pittsburgh, but Harrisburg afforded us a lovely life.

Our three children played together so well. David, Felicia, and Greg were so close in age that they functioned as three peas in a pod. They were known to raise Cain too. Once, someone contacted me with suspicions of the kids' involvement in disrupting a nearby Girl Scout camp. A group had rifled through the girls' belongings when they were on a hike, and apparently the Robb children were the number one suspects. I defended them, saying no way would my angelic children do something like that. Each played innocent until one of them confessed that they were indeed responsible.

I tell people who want to have three kids to try to have the boys on either end. Felicia was always the peacemaker. Whenever an uproar started, she was the angel and the boys were caught red-handed. David and Greg would always get annoyed that I would go "soft" on Felicia. Peg and I were blessed with the three of them. When there was a need for discipline, I'd say Peg was the "mental disciplinarian" and I the "physical."

Peg would say, "Something has to happen here," and I'd step in. We didn't spank them though. They would lose privileges for acting out, like going to bed early or not being able to watch TV. Peg gets the credit for bringing the kids up so well. As the children grew, I would note to myself how amazing Peg handled everything after her postpartum depression. I had seen her in her absolute worst time, and she held things together so well.

Peg and I presented a united front as parents, but in central Pennsylvania we both grew a little concerned that the kids were far removed from the city life we had known.

In Mechanicsburg on Sundays, Peg would walk the kids to the one traffic light in town and teach them to follow the red and green signals. That was their one opportunity to learn any kind of street smarts. Looking back, it's clear that she was doing her best to teach them how to live where she eventually wanted to move: a city.

All three kids went to Harrisburg Academy, a private school attended by the children of many state politicians. In those Harrisburg years, Peg also had an opportunity to pursue further education. Attending college had been her lifelong dream. She found a distance-learning program at Goddard College in Vermont, and for two or three months every summer, she took classes on campus toward a Humanities degree. When Peg would go to Vermont, the kids would stay home with me, or more often, vacation with Mother and Bob at their Connecticut home. I'm sure they preferred the cuisine of Mother's cook to mine—my dinners always involved some version of corned beef hash.

Peg was quite a conservative person, but a different part of her life opened up like a book at Goddard. Most of the students were younger. I don't think Peg minded that she was among the oldest. She met people there who she adored, and they saw her as a sage older sister. Many of Peg's classmates were working artists without families, with lifestyles far different from ours in Harrisburg. They saw Peg as a therapist and poured out their troubles to her.

I think the influence of her classmates encouraged her to dream of a career in the arts. Once she finished her degree, for example, she took a job at a Harrisburg classical music radio station as a deejay. She had the most wonderful, soothing voice. Her shift was early in the morning, and I remember driving the kids to school and their wanting to listen to a certain station that had a popular, comical deejay in the morning.

"But we've got to listen to mom!" I would say.

That college degree did wonders for Peg; it opened up all sorts of doors and strengthened her self-esteem. By then Peg had met a lot of my Yale classmates and noticed how well-educated all of the wives were. She would compare herself and tell me she felt uncomfortable in their midst. I couldn't believe it. I told her people didn't look at her that way.

Repeatedly I would say, "Look, you stack up with them. There is no reason you have to feel this way. Some people go to college and don't know enough to come in out of the rain."

She wouldn't listen.

The Central Pennsylvania Yale Club got quite a kick out of the fact that I had a wife who went to Goddard, a very left-wing avant-garde college at the time. But I couldn't have been happier for Peg. For years she corresponded with a few of her classmates and some of her favorite professors.

⁙ 53 ⁙

About a year after we moved to Harrisburg, Johnny Heinz contacted me. He was interested in running for office. Equipped with good credentials and a significant bankroll, Heinz was beginning the trajectory that would end in his becoming a US senator. I could tell that he wanted me to take a senior campaign position. I was very frank about the fact that I didn't want to be anyone's assistant anymore.

I had been in politics long enough to learn that many people fell into the role of "hangers-on," assistants who get so caught up in the thrill of campaigning that they hesitate to make a break, always concerned how far their candidate's ascension might take them.

"John, my way is not to be at that end of politics," I said before he offered me any role. I didn't want to have to turn him down. He was a nice guy, a Yale alum, and we got along well.

My role for the governor would shift soon as well. About 18 months after we arrived in Harrisburg, Ray Shafer confronted me with one of the most important decisions of my professional life. Cliff Jones, the man who had served as secretary of labor, was very ill. Would I step into the role?

"You've done all this work behind the scenes," Shafer said, "It's time to get yourself up front."

I would be the youngest person ever appointed to that position. The job would be more Herculean than I could imagine. Labor and Industry is the largest government entity in Harrisburg, and as such, I would have a significant number of employees answering to me. I agreed to the nomination.

I'll never forget the swearing-in ceremony. Harry Boyer, my colleague from Scranton's Human Rights Commission, a staunch Democrat, and the head of the AFL/CIO union, came to show his approval. His presence said a lot about my efforts and abilities to bring bipartisan support to the job, regardless of my lack of experience.

The local news covered the ceremony, and I couldn't wait to watch it with Peg that night. I especially wanted to watch an interview I had given. So Peg and I got the kids into their rooms and turned on one of those bulky, old-style televisions. Mesmerized, I watched the segment and then turned to Peg for her reaction. She had fallen asleep.

"Peg!" I called. "Peg, you missed it!"

David heard me and hollered down the hallway, "It's great, Dad! You did great!"

⁑ 54 ⁑

My agenda as secretary of Labor and Industry for the Commonwealth was driven by the labor promises that Shafer had made on his "14 Points" campaign. What surprised me most, I think, was the political nature of the work environment.

Most employees of L&I were civil service appointees to positions that existed for the best interests of the state (as opposed to Republican or Democrat nominees). But I found out quickly that Labor and Industry most definitely had a "red team" and a "blue team." Depending upon the elected governor's party, the affiliated team would take charge of activities and agendas. Never was this stated directly. After elections, people eased in and out of certain roles. It's a bit hard to articulate, especially as I could never quite understand why this happened. It was a silent and passive/aggressive maneuvering. I didn't like it one bit and tried to squash this thinking. Nothing kills progress more than this type of governance.

I never tried to apologize for my age or lack of experience. Roles in politics can and do change so quickly. Overnight, I had gone from a consultancy protested by Democrats in the legislature to becoming secretary of labor. The days of the Ford Edsel were long gone, replaced by a car, driver, and PR adviser. I knew that the most important thing I could do was show that I cared about the people and wanted to do the job set before me. The only conversations I wanted to have were about the job, not my age or resumé.

As a Fuller Brush man, I had at least one visit with a mentor salesman to teach me the ropes. At L&I, I had no option to shadow anyone. Shafer had an outstanding Cabinet. It really worked like a team, and individuals there kept me informed. I also had division heads, so I made sure that we met regularly and that I listened to them. More than anything, I didn't want to come across like a "Johnny know it all" trailblazer. I wanted to convince people that I had a real interest in doing my job without trying to overplay my role. Step by step, I took on one issue at a time and made sure there were no holes in the boat, so to speak. Eventually, people trusted me enough to share their hang-ups. Never did I worry about winning them over.

As governor, Shafer had as hard a time getting things passed by Republicans as he did Democrats. Part of the problem was that he had to find a way to pay for initiatives begun by Bill Scranton, and many legislators disapproved of his budget allocations (even though I'm sure they privately understood them). It was Shafer who proposed the state's first income tax to benefit Pennsylvania's education and public assistance spending. This turned into something of a political disaster.

Budget meetings were often tense. At one serious meeting with leaders of the House and the Senate, I decided to bring a little levity to the discussion.

"I've got the answer," I said. "Let's just lease Pittsburgh to Ohio and sell Philadelphia to New Jersey." Some laughed, but not as many as I had hoped. And Shafer just stared at me.

The governor knew, though, that I had made some very good friends on both sides of the aisle. He asked me to help get votes where he needed them. I remember helping with two workers compensation bills in particular. For one, I found more Democrat votes than Republican, and it passed without trouble. The other issue was more complex. I could only get about half of what the governor wanted. I remember going to his office to admit my failings.

He put his arm around me and said, "You've got 50 percent of what I wanted, and that's progress." I was flabbergasted. Rarely had I heard of someone saying something like this. In today's world, missing the boss's mark often sounds like, "You can take the highway if you don't get 100 percent approval." That gesture meant so much to me. I'll never forget it.

Unemployment compensation was a hot topic in Pennsylvania during those years. People were always at loggerheads over that one. Eventually, we put out most of those fires and got our financial system back in order. I was there when we finally managed to get "miner's disease," or black lung, included in the compensation. That was a challenge and a half.

These worthy initiatives cost money, and one way that we paid for them was to defund certain offices throughout the Commonwealth. I made sure that the press secretary published a list of offices that I intended to close along with a note encouraging legislators to meet with me if they wanted to appeal. One representative did just that. He came and gave me all the reasons why the office in his district needed to stay open. So I gave it another review and came back to him and said, "Sorry, I think we're doing the right thing."

He told a reporter that he did not approve of my shutting down the office and was going to make me "eat my words." This irked me.

So I invited him to my office at Labor and Industry to negotiate the dispute. He showed up ready to tear me apart. After he sat down, I had an aide come in with a plate, knife, and fork. My directive to close the office sat on the plate.

I looked at the man and said, "I want to be ready in case I have to eat my words."

That guy had no idea what to do. He just stared, then started laughing. He didn't know what to say. My staff just loved that episode.

RAY SHAFER WAS DETERMINED TO IDENTIFY AND REMOVE static programs, antiquated laws, and any red tape that kept citizens from accessing their rights. He was so committed to this ideology that as soon as he took office, he called for a Constitutional Convention in which all of the laws of the Commonwealth were reviewed. Critics accused Shafer of hoping to revise the rules of his own office, perhaps even extending the number of years that a governor might serve. But Shafer had anticipated this. To get the proposal past the legislature, he said he would limit himself to one term and refuse to seek reelection. That worked.

The Constitutional Convention became a highlight of Shafer's tenure and perhaps the high point of his political career. It wasn't enough, though, to realize the passage of his most forward-thinking bill: gun control. We were confident that we had enough votes in the House and the Senate to pass this necessary measure, but at the last minute, a conversation with the NRA collapsed and the bill failed. Shafer's team came within a whisker of what would have been landmark legislation in Pennsylvania.

More than anything else, Shafer's push to introduce a state income tax turned Pennsylvania over to the Democrats. His successor, Milton Shapp, was the state's first Jewish governor and the first Pennsylvania governor to serve two terms (the Constitutional Convention called by Shafer authorized the opportunity for governors to serve successive terms). He was also the first governor to propose a state income tax. Shafer's thinking had been spot-on. He had sharp instincts but lacked the widespread support he needed to pull off controversial ideas.

After leaving the gubernatorial seat, Shafer became a candidate for the Pennsylvania Supreme Court. Shot down by Republican chairman Billy Meehan, he couldn't get enough votes. Ranking Republicans could have come to Shafer's assistance but didn't. It was really sad.

By then, Richard Nixon had finally made it into the Oval Office by defeating Johnson's vice president, Hubert Humphrey, in 1968. President Nixon named Shafer the head of his National Commission on Marijuana and Drug Abuse. In this role for what became known as the "Shafer Commission," Shafer and his team recommended the decriminalization of marijuana, a decision that shocked Republicans across the country. By then, I was too busy fending off lots of L&I challenges in Philadelphia to follow that story closely.

Shafer's children told *The New York Times* upon his death that Nixon had wanted their father to be his running mate in the 1968 election. Shafer turned it down, they said, because he didn't trust Nixon. The *Times* was unable to confirm this story that would have placed Shafer in the role that went to Spiro Agnew, and eventually future president Gerald Ford.

I can easily say that Ray Shafer was one of the finest people I ever met. I benefited greatly from his advice and counsel.

⁖ 55 ⁖

Governor Milton Shapp had a hard time gaining Senate approval for his appointment to succeed me. For one year, I served a second governor in this role. There wasn't any shift in the Labor and Industry agenda, and I had a good enough rapport with Democrats. So I changed my resumé to say that I served as secretary of labor under two governors.

As I went through the motions of the job until Shapp received approval for my replacement, I spent time researching my next professional steps. I'm sure Peg dreamed of heading back to New York, and, of course, Mother and Bob wanted us to return. Mom and Bob were amazed that one governor had appointed me to do anything—much less two. I'm sure that Bob thought I was living in some kind of dream sequence.

The kids were happy at home and at Harrisburg Academy and very proud of their dad's work. To them, the most important part of my job involved elevator maintenance. Each elevator in Pennsylvania had a little cabinet inside of it with a sign that read, "This elevator has been inspected by…" and then a picture of me as representative of the Labor Department. Every time the kids entered an elevator, they would, to my embarrassment, open the little door to see my photo and say, "That's my dad."

I think the kids would have been pleased to spend the rest of their childhood in Harrisburg. But Peg knew even before I did that we were not about to settle in central Penn-sylvania. If we didn't want to become a suburban family, then we needed to make a move.

⸱ 56 ⸱

One day I unexpectedly received a call from a David Maxwell, who also had attended Yale before becoming Shafer's secretary of insurance. When his state Cabinet position ended, Maxwell accepted the role of chief lawyer to George Romney, President Nixon's secretary of Housing and Urban Development.

Maxwell told me that Romney was looking for someone to take over HUD's office in Philadelphia, where he suspected malfeasance. Maxwell had recommended me, and after my name had floated in a pool with a couple of others, found its way to the top of the list.

Would I be interested, Maxwell asked, in interviewing with George Romney in Washington?

The interview went very well, but there was a hurdle to clear with Republican Senator Hugh Scott, who needed to approve me for the position. Scott had an aide who wasn't at all thrilled with my candidacy. He was the type that I hadn't wanted to become—somebody so firmly entrenched in being an assistant to power that he assumed airs of the office himself. Maxwell helped me with such bumps in the road, and soon all the right people who needed to support me as the HUD regional administrator for Region 3 did. Romney named me as head of the Philadelphia office.

When I first started the job, the family stayed in Harrisburg. Once again, I wasn't sure what to expect, and I didn't want to uproot the kids in the middle of a school year. So during the week I lived in Center City at the Ben Franklin Hotel, walked every day to my office at the Curtis Center, and on weekends commuted back to Harrisburg. After five to six months of that, I was ready for everyone to relocate. So was Peg. We both saw a wealth of opportunities for the children in the city. Several months at HUD in the early 1970s also awakened me to the white flight that was rapidly changing urban demographics. I had a terrible feeling that many of those fleeing were escaping something they didn't understand.

I'll never forget telling Mother and Bob that we were moving the kids to Philadelphia. They hit the roof. They very much would have agreed with Donald Trump, that "bad things happen in Philadelphia." Mother thought the town was seedy and the center of sin. I don't know exactly why Philadelphia had such a negative connotation in Mother's circles. It sounds funny, but I think even the name bothered her. It was longer than Boston, Baltimore, or Washington. "*Phil-a-del-phi-a!*" she would draw out with a brusque tone.

Once I accepted the role at HUD, Bob Ellinger finally stopped pressing me about becoming a Wall Street broker. He could tell my professional future for the time being was in government work. But both he and Mother would have been happy seeing me commute to a suburban setting for the rest of my HUD career. They thought I was endangering my family and ruining my children's academic prospects.

But move to Philadelphia we certainly did. I found a rental on Sixth and Spruce Street in Society Hill. The neighborhood had taken a dive but was coming back to life, and Washington Square Park was a decent place for the kids to play. Peg and I enrolled all three at St. Mary's Interparochial School. Having had a top-notch privileged education at

Harrisburg Academy, they had quite a transition into St. Mary's. Peg had always wanted them to have a Catholic education. While we had several schools to choose from, St. Mary's was quite diverse, offering generous scholarships to low-income students. Each of the children eventually made good friends there. I think if David, Felicia, and Gregory could have chosen for themselves, they would have stayed in Harrisburg. But this was a good challenge for them, albeit socially more than academically.

We all loved our rental house. After a couple of years, the owner offered to sell it to us for an astronomical price. It would have been quite a stretch. The offer prompted me to start looking at real estate, but there wasn't much in our price range. Before and during my search, I had taken to imagining the family living in a particular house on South Seventh Street that I passed every day on my walk to work and liked the look of. It wasn't for sale, but my realtor reached out to the owner anyway. He learned the man was hoping to rehab and sell it for a profit. After putting on a new roof, he fell into financial straits. I heard this and immediately offered him $60,000, a lot of money at the time, but far less than the Spruce Street owner had asked. Soon 236 Seventh Street became our new home. I can truly say that we moved into the house of my dreams. But it would need a lot of work.

⚜ 57 ⚜

Mother and Bob weren't the only ones concerned about the family's safety in Philadelphia. Some of our children's friends lived in suburban Philadelphia, and their parents felt a bit wary bringing their kids into town for birthday parties and get-togethers. Good friends of ours, the Bedells, had moved to Philadelphia from Harrisburg just before we did, which allowed the kids to have a built-in social network as soon as we arrived. It was several of these children who lived in the suburbs.

I remember planning for a small caravan to come into town for one of David's birthday parties. One mother, in particular, was scared to death to have her son enter the city limits. She called and had me take out a map so she could stipulate the exact geographical area where her son could walk with her permission. I had planned to take the kids to a ballgame at one of the stadiums, and after I guaranteed her son's safety, she agreed to send him.

Seven children and I took a bus from our neighborhood to Pattison Avenue. Everything went fine until the return trip. I got on the bus and turned toward the kids, reminding them that we were going to stay together. Then I realized the kid with the fearful mother was standing on the sidewalk.

I had just enough time before the bus pulled away to yell out the window, "Take the next bus and get off at Locust! Remember Locust!"

Back at Broad and Locust, I sent our children home with their friends and waited quite some time for this kid to step off the next bus. He didn't show up. I went home and made the phone call that is every parent's nightmare.

"What did you say?" the boy's mother yelled into the phone.

"I've lost your son."

She told me I was in big trouble and threatened me up and down.

I had called my lawyer before I heard a knock at the door. There was the lost boy with a big smile on his face. He had gotten on the wrong bus but had enough smarts to walk up to the driver and say, "I'm supposed to get off at Broad and Locust." The driver dropped him off as close as he could along his route, and the kid had found his way back to our house. I could tell he had just had the time of his life.

Immediately I put him on the phone to his mother and everything eventually cooled down.

TRUTH BE TOLD, THERE HAVE BEEN A FEW TIMES WHEN I've felt threatened living in town. I'm a heavy sleeper but once heard someone break in through the front door. I scared them away by roaring down the stairs while making a lot of noise. Neighborhood robberies were a big problem in our first decade or two here. Thieves weren't looking for confrontations though.

Once a thief tried to break in through our back door, which is separated from the side street by a small lot and a fence. Friends of ours on Spruce Street happened to look out the window on their top floor and saw someone balancing on top of our fence. Thinking something terrible was about to happen, the wife told her husband to call 911.

"Oh no, the Robbs are just having a party," he responded.

Later I said to Peg, "What kind of reputation do we have?"

That time the burglar tried to break in through the kitchen window. Hearing him, I had enough time to call the police.

We did get invaded once when we went to visit cousins in Virginia. I hadn't locked the back gate, and a couple of thieves broke in through the back door. A neighbor called and said to return right away. The damage done was evident from outside. The group had destroyed and stolen quite a bit from our first floor and basement. They hadn't gone upstairs, I'm sure, for fear they'd be caught.

A few nights later, I heard a thumping and rushed to the window. Two guys were trying to break in next door. I called the police and they were caught.

Peg and I added a second lock on the front door and took other security measures.

I did spend some sleepless nights here though, that's for sure.

❖ 58 ❖

In my attic office, I have a framed letter that Richard Nixon signed in 1971. It contains my official appointment as Regional Administrator, Mid-Atlantic Region of the United States Department of Housing and Urban Development. My territory of responsibility included not only Philadelphia and Delaware, but also Baltimore, Virginia, West Virginia, Maryland, and Washington, DC.

For all of his flaws, Nixon was astute and knew how to make the federal government work. His administration pushed for all sorts of things that wouldn't be traditionally associated with Republicans today, including Section 8 housing subsidies and the Environmental Protection Agency. Nixon had foresight. For example, he formed regional councils that helped to unify various federal agencies located in every region. I became the chairman of the Federal Regional Council in Philadelphia. Our council included the departments of Health and Human Services, Welfare, the Environmental Protection Agency, and HUD. When tragedy did strike, we administrators already knew one another and could more readily accelerate needed services to the public. Structured interagency response isn't, unfortunately, typical for federal organizations.

I always had a harder time communicating with people in Washington than I did with any number of difficult personalities in Philadelphia. My territory was referred to as Region 3, and within it was a HUD office in Washington, DC. It was quite awkward from an organizational standpoint because central office secretaries and assistants constantly tried to push their agendas directly on the Washington office.

Fortunately, I was familiar with bureaucracies. Early on, I recognized the conflict and said to my Washington head, "Listen, just keep me posted on things you're being asked to do. You won't have to worry about my saying you are wrong."

This isn't to say that things were easy in Philadelphia.

When George Romney selected me for the office, the mandate was "to clean it up." I didn't know exactly what that meant, but I did know I wasn't hired for my housing intelligence: that was limited to the basic understanding of my mortgage. The idea was that I would root out any malfeasance in the office, and then someone else would succeed me.

For years, Federal Housing Authority appraisers in Philadelphia had been accepting illegal and unethical payoffs from developers and contractors. The bribes most likely began, but certainly multiplied, when sellers (usually developers who had purchased properties dirt cheap) wanted appraisals to reflect higher market values. These developers were mostly based in New York City and would pay off government employees with cash or expensive dinners in Manhattan. The appraisers would then inflate their assessments. They got away with it until the "white flight" of the mid-20th century drew attention to real estate and journalists focused the spotlight on these types of fraudulent transactions.

A couple of high-profile FHA appraisals had drawn press because of the degree to which they had been enhanced, and when I arrived, HUD was trying to manage the blowback. The office at the time had quite a split. On the one side were young idyllic employees in bell-bottoms doing exciting work with redevelopment and urban renewal. On the other side was FHA, staffed by much older employees whose only job was to insure mortgages. Quite a lot of resentment had developed between the two groups: the old guard at FHA considered themselves the basis for HUD, and the younger urban renewal planners condemned unethical FHA practices that put money in developers' hands at the expense of those who badly needed housing.

When I started poking my nose around FHA, I was greeted with quite a bit of resentment. Once again, I didn't really understand the business but had training in the bureaucracy. My approach was the same as it had been in Harrisburg—to show that I cared about people and wanted to do the job as well as I could to benefit the public.

I decided to hold a meeting with the appraisers and the major housing developers in one room. I wasn't afraid to call the shots. These hustlers could sense there would be no beating around the bush. At the meeting's start, I could see them looking at one another with consternation.

"I've found some very bad things going on," I said. Then I directed my comments to the developers. "You all are providing funds for appraisers and taking them on special trips, and it's going to stop."

They were shocked. I always had this feeling that the contractors thought, "This out-of-town hayseed. We can play his organ and tie him up in knots!" They didn't realize that I had a lot of experience and could cut through the bullshit.

As for the appraisers, they had spent enough time justifying things that they had come to see extra handouts as their God-given right. They had been an island unto themselves.

In no time, complaints about me reached Romney's office and I got a phone call summoning me to Washington. Romney's office didn't want me to rattle the age-old FHA cage because of the long support that had flowed between it and HUD. I was told to keep a low profile. I reminded the powers that be that they had hired me for one reason only—to get rid of malfeasance. They had been prepared to give me some room because they knew I had to address bad stuff, but I think they thought I would take my time. I wanted it gone immediately.

My predecessor, I learned, had a knack for urban renewal but was somewhat afraid of the FHA situation. He approached the job as if he were a professional HUD employee and not a political appointee. I think he also was bored, having been there a number of years. After his forced resignation, the office had been vacant for about six months before my arrival, time enough for things to spiral more quickly out of control.

It took me about six more months to root out most of the corruption. Fortunately, I had a team of government watch-dogs to call in, and they greatly helped my investigation. Based on their recommendations, I fired quite a few people. I shook up the morning routines of more. People had gotten used to coming in fifteen, twenty, even thirty minutes late for work every day. To set a tone of no-nonsense, I knew this had to stop as well. So I moved my desk directly in front of the elevator. As soon as the door opened, latecomers would see me and I them. I never had to say anything. Within two weeks, everyone came to work on time.

I became persona non grata at FHA. Quickly appraisers started planting stories about my taking money from developers. After a couple of phone calls to the IRS, the agency decided to review my taxes, as they did every year for a few years. The woman I dealt with was very funny, as I recall. One year, she pointed out an error I had made that resulted in my getting a chunk of money back from the government. Another complaint went directly to Secretary Romney. There was a developer named Herb Barness who was closely associated with the Philadelphia Eagles. He had repeatedly offered me tickets as a gift, and repeatedly I had said no. Then an envelope full of tickets arrived for me and the kids. I called Barness's secretary and asked her to name a charity that he supported. I found out the value of the tickets, then made the same contribution in kind to the charity.

Pretty soon, the rumor mill carried the story that I was taking tickets as a payoff from Barness. Romney had always had my back, and after hearing my explanation over the phone, he said it was best to send someone from the inspector general's office to Philadelphia to investigate the story. I understood. I called Barness and told him that he was going to be investigated as well.

After his interview, he called me back, laughing. At the end of the investigation—which cleared me of any wrongdoing—the inspector general's man had the gall to ask Barness for free Eagles tickets to the upcoming game.

❖ 59 ❖

I thought I would be head of Philadelphia's HUD office for about a year. I ended up staying for four. The challenges of the job fascinated me, and once I started learning about Section 8, which began almost as soon as I took office, I felt called to the work.

Throughout most of Nixon's administration, HUD flourished. Housing studies conducted as part of FDR's New Deal program developed strength during the civil rights movement, and one result was government-subsidized housing, otherwise known as "Section 8." Public housing had existed prior to Section 8, but the program involved courting the private sector so that private developers could build properties to help people.

Housing rose to the top of the president's agenda, and for a time, Congress funded HUD quite a bit. Thrilled about the program, I found myself a lone voice in worrying over the limits of the government's largesse. I remember being called to Washington for a special briefing on Section 8 before it was publicly announced. As I listened to the presentation, I wondered how the government was planning to control the cost, as it seemed quite open-ended. Based on Philadelphia's needs alone, I knew necessary funding would skyrocket.

I put up my hand. "Has anybody looked at the fact that this is going to be something that grows incrementally in terms of cost?"

Of course, nobody wanted to hear of a potential problem at such an exciting time. I was cautioned to be a cheerleader and not ask these kinds of questions.

Section 8 spawned so many more things we could do for people. The federal government assigned dollars to HUD that we could use to fund our housing programs. Developers loved this and approached us with all sorts of proposals. Section 8 contracts became very competitive. Affordable housing is not a lucrative business, but developers wanted in on it so that they had a shot at controlling this promising market. Everyone wanted their projects approved. If our team saw a project application for a location where there was no need for housing, we would say, "Go somewhere where there is more poverty." Once we approved a location, we would haggle with the developer over the number of units the neighborhood needed, how many could be developed, and then get into more minutiae, like bedroom size.

Never before had I understood the ill-housed conditions of low-income people. To better understand the demands on HUD, and to get a full sense of the city's needs, I visited as many properties as I could. The situation was appalling. A big part of the work became educating people on the basics of living in a house. Many just didn't know how to handle it because they had never lived in one before. For example, people put all kinds of things down the toilet. How do you teach people of a certain age not to do that without insulting them?

We had to find a way to prepare people to live in homes of their own. In Harrisburg, I had done some housing work as secretary of labor. So I knew to develop relationships with educational entities and ask them how to best help low-income individuals and families make transitions from shelters and the streets into housing. We decided to spend months at the outset taking people through mandatory classes that respectfully educated them before they moved into their properties. This helped.

Section 8 was a true success. It did exactly what it intended to do: help people who desperately needed housing find affordable places to live. The problem is that now it has become a disparaging phrase. The program started unraveling a few years after it started. I had identified the reason when nobody had wanted to listen. Without a cap, Section 8 had become outrageously expensive. Nobody had ever dreamed that Section 8 would become so successful, and momentum would only grow.

Soon after Nixon's reelection, all HUD regional directors got a memo from Secretary Romney's office that essentially stated, "As of next week, you will fund no new commitments for Section 8 projects." It also said that applications submitted prior to this memo could be considered.

I consulted with my staff and made them aware of this loophole. We had quite a few applications waiting to be considered. With future funding on the cutting block, developers had escalated their pressure to fund our Region 3 pipeline.

I felt so strongly about housing that I wanted as many commitments as possible on the street. The month following the memo, the Philadelphia office secured more development commitments and housing projects than any other region.

I got a call from Washington.

"Ted," Secretary Romney's deputy director said, "you didn't read the message the way you were supposed to read it."

Instead of killing the program, I had advanced it. I listened to them tell me that I didn't follow orders correctly, but I didn't care. I kept thinking to myself, "Hey, I am in the business of housing." I thought it was a bad decision to try to shortcut these projects. So did my colleagues throughout the country. More than one other director called me and said they wished they had done the same thing.

Once again, I can't help but repeat that I had more difficulties with the layer of undersecretaries around Secretary Romney than with community activists. They wanted control, resented whoever threatened their notions, and worked to make the situation more difficult.

Take away government subsidies for affordable housing, and all you are doing is developing properties for people at market value, which means low-income people will end up paying most of their meager salaries on rent. This is largely the reason for tent encampments in Philadelphia and other places. The government has strangled Section 8 by refusing to maintain and provide the necessary funding for affordable housing. For all intents and purposes, the program was finished. And I don't see how it will come back to form. Of all the departments, HUD had the weakest committee support in Washington. Its decline started at the end of the Nixon era and received the death knell under President George W. Bush.

Then, of course, about four years ago Trump named a brain surgeon to run the department.

⁖ 60 ⁖

I think the most difficult person I ever dealt with in office was Philadelphia Mayor Frank Rizzo. He hated the idea of affordable housing, especially in his beloved South Philadelphia neighborhoods.

Some communities simply didn't want us on their blocks. They feared the people that affordable housing would bring. Rizzo supported this type of arrogant thinking. We got into fracas after fracas over project proposals for South Philly. He didn't want his people "infected" by the miserable human beings that his constituents feared we would set upon them.

I remember one project in particular that the South Philly community was dead set against. At the time, I had a deputy named Vince Marino, a political friend of Rizzo's from South Philadelphia. Marino was a loyal worker but no pushover. A Democrat, he became my deputy over harsh objections from Washington. I remember saying, "I don't care how he votes as long as he remains loyal to pursuing our office initiatives." He gave me invaluable input and advice. Repeatedly he would play the devil's advocate with me, even outright disagreeing, but we worked well together. Marino helped me engage these South Philly neighborhoods, and I'm sure he went to bat for me with Rizzo.

The atmosphere surrounding this upcoming initiative was so volatile that Marino and I called a community meeting. It was more contentious than I had anticipated. Before its start, I conducted a little research and determined that many of the people complaining lived in low-rise housing projects with federal (FHA) assistance.

I proposed a solution.

"The community activists can sell their FHA-funded properties back to the government and then move into the new high rise."

Oh, did they hate me for saying that. But I accomplished my objective—to point out their hypocrisy and racism. They were benefiting from government help. They just didn't want HUD's Black clientele to have the same opportunity.

Time after time Rizzo would call when he heard of such projects and try to stop them. Occasionally he succeeded. Most of the time we could fend off his disapproval. The only agency he despised more than HUD perhaps was the EPA. The mayor had no time or respect for them either.

Rizzo knew that ultimately he had to deal with me, especially after President Nixon started the regional council and named me as the head. That made me one of the more senior federal officials in Philadelphia. At the same time, though, Rizzo had the president's ear. Nixon wanted the Democratic mayor's nomination when it came time for reelection in 1972. The president valued people according to their political capital, and Rizzo had plenty of it. Should Rizzo endorse him, Nixon knew, Democratic Philadelphia would be able to follow suit. Nixon was so intent on getting Rizzo's approval that he invited the mayor to the White House.

It must have been George Romney who directed me to attend this White House meeting. He wanted me in the room when the two talked as he was fearful of what Rizzo might recall the president had promised him. Rizzo was the kind of guy who could stretch the truth, and I was considered to be a member of a truth squad, so to speak.

The mayor and I met outside the Oval Office. There was no traveling into town together, coffee beforehand, or lunch afterward. We both understood the situation. Privately I wondered if he might use the occasion to argue some of the disagreements we had over affordable housing. I wouldn't have put it past him to try to get Nixon to take his side in a twenty-minute "meet and greet" moment. But it didn't come up.

The entire time, Rizzo looked like he had died and gone to heaven. I had never seen the mayor so bewitched. The president was very friendly under the circumstances. He had Rizzo's number, but he knew he was forging an alliance and it was in his best interest to give Rizzo the time of day. It was like watching some kind of mutual admiration society.

BACK IN PHILADELPHIA, RIZZO LEVERAGED HIS NOMINA-tion wisely, which made life a little more hellish for me. The word was out among the Republican leadership: "Don't anger Frank Rizzo." He and I continued to get into fracases, and occasionally one would develop in the newspapers. A reader of the Philadelphia, New York, and Baltimore daily papers, Secretary Romney would learn of the infighting. More than once Dave Maxwell called to advise me to lower my profile.

During one mayoral news conference, an assistant of mine challenged a statement that Rizzo made to the press. It had to do with his disapproval of yet another housing project.

The assistant had raised his hand in the meeting to let the mayor know that the project would indeed go forward as it had all of the necessary approvals.

Rizzo took the comment as a personal affront and called the White House. Soon I got a call directing me that I had twenty-four hours to reassign my employee.

It isn't easy to fire a civil servant. There is a process. In fact, there was a paragraph written into law that to fire a civil servant, someone had to file multiple actions against them, filings that required meetings, and the presence of somebody of the civil servant's rank or higher to represent him or her.

Not only was I incensed that Rizzo had gone over my head, but also that I would have to come up with paperwork that documented my guy's abuse of office, which didn't exist. Had the mayor called me, I could have had the opportunity to explain my position: my assistant, in a way, was trying to save the mayor from making a foolish error. The project approvals were in, and he didn't want Rizzo proclaiming some outcome that was not about to happen. But now I had Nixon saying fire away.

I called my counterpart, Bill Green, the HUD administrator for the New York office, and learned he needed a director for Camden. I told Bill that my guy would be great for the role, and Green agreed. Instead of demoting or firing the worker, I had found a way to promote him.

I remember calling him in on a Friday.

"You're reporting to Camden on Monday," I said. "You're taking over the office. Please don't ask me any questions."

He was smart enough to understand things like this didn't happen so quickly.

Boy, did Rizzo piss me off that time. I find it very interesting and appropriate that his legacy has been tarnished now that the Black Lives Matter movement has sparked inquiry into the history of his racist views and behavior. His popularity was due to his ability to connect with a specific middle- and lower-class white segment of the population. Yes, he was a Democrat, but not very many Democratic leaders at the time embraced him. It's interesting to think about that now.

I've been a city resident through many Democratic mayors since Frank Rizzo. I was a particular fan of Ed Rendell; in the 1990s he represented a real turning point for the party. It was Rendell whose charisma and passion for the city helped residents see what they could accomplish by working together. The man used to be a constant presence at fundraising events, and as a result, almost everybody spoke of him as a mayor who really cared about his people.

I've had conversations I think with every mayor since moving to Philadelphia in the early 1970s. This was business-related at first, and then my name somehow found a spot on prospective fundraising lists.

Ted Robb

⸲ 61 ⸲

The perspicacity of Nixon's regional administration council became apparent when Hurricane Agnes engulfed the Scranton/Wilkes-Barre area. At the time, Agnes was the most severe hurricane to hit the United States—and the costliest—ultimately resulting in over $2 billion in damage. Pennsylvania, ironically, received the brunt of the storm. The hurricane caused major flooding along the Susquehanna and Lackawanna rivers, and metropolitan Scranton and Wilkes-Barre were devastated. Harrisburg was badly damaged as well.

As the most senior man in the regional council, I became chairman of the task force to spearhead recovery. For about eight months, I was dispatched to Scranton and traveled all over the center part of the state.

The first thing I did was contact all elected officials. I told them that I was there to provide services, and if they had particular needs for their constituents, they could contact me directly. Some took me up on that. It was a pain to get a phone call every five minutes, but I thought it quite important to establish that connection to the people. So often in situations like that—as we saw during the aftermath of Hurricane Katrina in New Orleans—individuals just don't know who to contact.

George Romney took a personal interest in aiding recovery, and as a result, the Red Cross and FEMA deployed teams immediately. Romney's presence at our weekly meetings was instrumental in helping Pennsylvania get the relief money it so desperately needed.

The hardest part of the job was aiding the people who lived near the river and had their entire homes washed away. And flood insurance wasn't something that many families had. Many of these flood victims wanted our financial assistance to rebuild their homes on their original homesteads at the same site that had been devastated, a site where flood insurance continued to be unavailable.

Others had properties that weren't completely demolished and didn't want to leave them. This caused quite a bit of concern. We discussed whether it was worth investing federal money in rebuilding or whether we should force people to relocate. Of course, people did not want to relocate. We're all that way, aren't we? We all want to go back to where we started.

We were able to get the government to provide insurance and that helped a little bit, but we told many locals that they couldn't rebuild at the disaster site. Again and again, politicians barked at us and people told reporters, "Some government type is keeping me from continuing to reside in my flood-ravished home."

Being the point person for the Hurricane Agnes recovery was one of the biggest challenges of my life. I can't say enough about George Romney's presence and support. Having someone from the president's Cabinet in your court is a true game-changer. Romney was highly respected by all. Had he run for president, he very well may have carried the Republican nomination over Nixon in the election that Kennedy won in 1960. Romney's downfall was his criticism of Vietnam. After a trip to Asia, he publicly stated that he had been brainwashed into supporting the war. This put him at odds with key members of the party.

I came to idolize Romney. He had a great capacity for hearing a problem and immediately exploring resolutions. He would have made a great president. But when his Vietnam comments left him in the dust, he stood by the party and supported Nixon. Nixon always looked at people in terms of their political strength, so he rewarded Romney by appointing him to his Cabinet.

Romney left HUD before I did. He departed at the start of Nixon's second term in January 1973, about six months after the events that led to the Watergate scandal and over a year before Nixon's resignation. Upon leaving, Romney didn't hide his frustration with the president. He said that he didn't have much respect for those in office who didn't prioritize the biggest needs of the people. Everybody knew this was a thinly veiled criticism of Nixon.

Nixon wasn't easy to get along with, and he had high-profile clashes with several in his administration, including Romney, who felt the president tightening HUD's budget without justification. When I think about it, I wonder if Romney felt overwhelmed by the funding needs of Section 8 and government pressure to end parts of the program. It had flourished under his watch, and I wonder if he didn't want to deal with the politics that eventually would destroy it.

After he left office, Romney returned to Michigan and reentered private life. A lifelong advocate of volunteer efforts, he became the CEO of the National Center for Citizen Involvement, encouraging people to give back to their communities. His successor in Washington was a man named James Lynn, who bridged the gap between the fall of Nixon and the inauguration of Gerald Ford.

⁙ 62 ⁙

The night that Richard Nixon resigned the presidency, August 8, 1974, I was scheduled to give a speech to the National Association of Housing Redevelopment Officers (NAHRO) in Erie, Pennsylvania. It was a big thing for me, and I had prepared an in-depth presentation. But then word arrived that the president would resign. I realized my talk was one I would never deliver. The president's speech was too consequential.

I still attended the meeting, as did many others, but when I stood up, I said, "I think everybody should be watching their television right now rather than listening to me. Good-bye."

That got me the biggest round of applause I have ever received.

WITH NIXON'S DEPARTURE, VICE PRESIDENT GERALD Ford took office. I have to wonder whether Romney would have stayed as HUD secretary had he known Nixon's presidency would end so abruptly. Both Ford and Romney were progressive Republicans and good friends.

I doubt that Romney would have approved of Ford's choice for secretary of Housing and Urban Development. The president appointed a lawyer named Carla Anderson Hills, a woman with no housing experience and an eye on rising through the ranks.

Hills, a Yale Law School graduate, was a US assistant attorney general in the Department of Justice. At some point she was mentioned as a candidate for a vacancy on the Supreme Court, but Ford nominated John Paul Stevens instead. Hills ended up serving as secretary of HUD for about two years, which meant she left the department a year after I did. She would later become the primary negotiator of NAFTA and chair of the Council on Foreign Relations.

Hills and I did not get along very well. At one of HUD's first regional meetings under her reign, I suggested that we regional administrators (there were eleven of us) have time to meet one another and discuss our successes and challenges. No professional development experience is more valuable than the exchange of ideas with one's peers. Others heartily agreed with my suggestion, and we had a sensational meeting. I had always felt that the director out in California had an easier time of things, and this gave me a chance to hear him share the problems he faced and how he overcame them.

We never had another such meeting. The powers that be surrounding Carla Hills thought that I was preparing a coup d'etat for regional directors to assume more authority. This was asinine. I had seen what good came from Nixon's regional council meetings across agencies. I just wanted to hear how other administrators handled their challenges. But Washington's paranoia ruined that good idea.

⸎ 63 ⸎

About a year after Ford took office, Peg got a call at home. It was the White House. As she handed the phone over, she said, "It's someone from the White House, and all they want is your money!"

I took the phone. A voice on the other end of the line said that President Ford and the First Lady wanted to stay at our house. I thought it was a joke and said so.

The voice gave me a number and urged me to call back and verify the source of the call. So I did. When the White House answered, I realized this was no joke.

Ford was preparing to debate Jimmy Carter at the Walnut Street Theater ahead of the 1976 presidential election, and he wanted to stay at a neighboring home instead of a fancy hotel. The idea was that Ford could show that he, like Jimmy Carter, was a man of the people. Should I agree, and our house meet Secret Service approval, the government would put our family up in a hotel the night in question.

I said okay. When I hung up, I told Peg that the Secret Service was scheduled to inspect our home the following morning at 8 a.m. She and the kids said I was being snookered. Nevertheless, we all spent the night cleaning the house until 1 a.m.

Felicia, David, and Greg were teenagers then, and I remember looking into their rooms to see if there was anything inappropriate in sight. David had a poster on the wall of a nude man sprinting across a field. It read, "Keep on streaking." Greg's room had a poster of a scantily clad starlet. I made both pictures come down.

The next day we learned we needn't have bothered staying up so late. The Secret Service hadn't realized that our home shared a wall with the adjacent house. Putting the president in such a location was against protocol, they said, as they couldn't control what happened on the other side of the wall. They asked if I could help secure a better location within the week.

At the time, I was president of the Society Hill Civic Association. I started calling our members to ask whether the president might stay at their homes.

"Yeah right, Ted," I heard again and again. I couldn't find a suitable place. Finally, Otto Haas agreed. He had a stand-alone property in the neighborhood and the Secret Service approved it. The night that President and Mrs. Ford stayed in the Haas house, the civic association held a cocktail party for them. After we gave them a replica of the Liberty Bell, I remember talking to Ford about the lengths my family had gone to clean our house, and he laughed and laughed, especially about the streaker poster. We had a wonderful back and forth. I found Ford to have an excellent sense of humor, and both he and Betty Ford were appreciative of our efforts.

⁖ 64 ⁖

When I took on the directorship of HUD, I planned to be in the job for about a year. I stayed for five, serving under Carla Hills for the final two. I'm surprised I stayed so long under her eye.

One of the things a political appointee is required to do during a change in administration is write a letter of resignation. The new administrator then has the option of accepting the letter or not. This can take quite some time, and Hills sure waited before accepting mine.

Hills knew that I wasn't the cheerleader type. To her, I qualified as an irritant because I asked a lot of questions. At the same time, she was aware that summarily dismissing me could backfire on her. I had become a fairly high-profile member of HUD because of two factors—my term as regional administrator and my success as director of the Philadelphia office, which produced more housing than most, if not all, other offices. But neither Hills nor I had much respect for the way we each did our jobs. I don't know if we ever agreed. In some ways, it was a long two years.

More than anything else, my HUD years taught me that persistence was the most important characteristic for any political appointee to have. I learned never to take the first answer, and to probe for the reason behind any answer. Most superiors hated this approach. They didn't want to have to explain themselves. This alone dampened any further political inkling I may have had.

Right before I turned forty, I realized it was time to resign. Hills and I had a phone call during which we exchanged our mutual dissatisfaction. I said I was fed up with HUD, and she said she was fed up with me. One way or another, I said, I wanted both of us to move on. I stated my reasons for leaving as gracefully as possible in a press interview.

"Anyone who serves as I have has no desire to become a career employee. I like the government and I feel there aren't enough people with concern—and who are capable—who serve in critical positions," I said in an interview with *The Philadelphia Inquirer*. "But a bureaucrat I am not. I'm afraid that if I stay too long, I could easily fall into that category."

Hills had offered to help me find a new job but I declined, even though I didn't know what I was going to do and would soon have three children in college at the same time. I had a vague notion, though, that I would continue in the field of affordable housing.

⁝ 65 ⁝

I was very happy to see my deputy director Vince Marino take over my position at HUD. In addition to helping me navigate difficult affairs with Frank Rizzo, Marino was the mind behind the city's handling of the lead paint issue, which had become a hot topic during my tenure. Before the late 1970s, lead-based paint was the primary type of paint used in homes, especially old homes. This proved deadly as little children put paint chips in their mouths. As lawsuits mounted, the city could no longer ignore the fact that this was happening, and public housing had to act. But we didn't know what to do. We tore down walls, stripped paint, repainted, relocated, and moved people, but we had no idea how to handle the larger issue of children becoming sick in the very homes we put them in.

Marino was the one who focused the challenge by narrowing our investigation to the years that lead-based paint had been introduced. We could then take whatever possible measures to improve affected properties and inform the tenants. But that was a big challenge.

Marino was an excellent successor. In the several years he had the office, we would meet monthly for lunch. (Sadly he died in his late forties of a heart attack.)

I WOULD SAY THE HARDEST TIME I HAD PROFESSIONALLY was in the six-month window of time after I left HUD. I knew that I could make it as a consultant, and I knew that I was passionate about helping people find housing, but I just didn't know how to do it. I made a ton of phone calls to my professional network, scheduled meetings, and slowly found my way through the confusion. But those were some difficult times. Peg and I were always on a budget, and she painstakingly had me and the kids record all of our expenditures in a family budget book. Asking Mother for financial help wasn't an option. I knew there was a Ryan inheritance eventually coming my way. Bob Ellinger had set up a trust, but I wouldn't receive a penny of it until Mother died. I just never wanted to ask my mother for money. She always wanted some kind of exchange, and I didn't want to risk involving Peg or the children in any type of arrangement.

Never did I regret leaving government employment when I did. It's like what I told my grandson, Jeffrey, when he said he wanted to be an actor. I was thrilled. But my advice was, "Give yourself a certain timeframe for something to happen." Then if it doesn't happen, move along. You have to. Theater, like politics, requires luck, and also being in the right place at the right time. I realized this during my time with Jack McGregor, which led to many of the opportunities Ray Shafer and Dave Maxwell offered me. I had a set period of time to figure things out, and if I didn't have a clear direction, I knew I would have to move on to a different place. My public-sector involvement came to an end when I left HUD. It was time to find new challenges.

In many businesses, the framework for advancement is quite clear—there is a professional ladder, a chairman at the top, and you can focus your rise on specific steps. There is none of that in politics. What there is, as I told Jeffrey, is the opportunity to meet a lot of people. I told him to keep a running list in his mind of those he could one day ask for advice. I had developed a cadre of people who could help plug me into a new professional path should my political career end, as it did. These weren't necessarily the kind of people I knew well, but the kind I could contact with an update of my status.

Within six months after leaving HUD, I started flipping through my Rolodex and making calls around town, letting people know what I was doing and where I would be. Slowly my reputation helped me find the type of consulting work I wanted. I had to be careful because as a former HUD director I could not assist in any projects that began during my tenure. Hyperaware of this contingency, I struggled to file papers for what would become my first consulting firm: Robb & Associates.

Soon after I left office, HUD had come up with a refinancing project that I thought was very promising. As I contacted developers and property owners throughout the city, I let them know about this project and asked if they might be interested in refinancing their apartments. They realized that I knew HUD programs like the back of my hand. For a consultant's fee, I led them through the process and started making a name for myself in real estate. I had an acquaintance who owned property off of Rittenhouse Square, and in exchange for using him as my lawyer, he rented me office space. Peggy was my secretary.

Once I got going, I built up a clientele pretty quickly. That amazed me. I realized that sometimes when you are in a job, you don't realize how other people are forming an assessment of you, and how they are looking at you. One project in particular illustrates this—it came to me early on.

An African American reverend in Wilmington, Delaware, wanted his historic church restored, and his congregation didn't have much money. The man, I remember, was blind, and he would go everywhere with his seeing-eye dog. For months he had made municipal contacts, trying to find someone who could help him secure HUD financing. The man was tenacious, unwilling to let any obstacle shift his focus. At some point, someone put him in touch with a HUD representative who had known me as the one-time director of the region. This man told the reverend that I was now working as a consultant, and I was able to go to Wilmington and help him work through the red tape. It was so much easier working in Delaware than Pennsylvania. The state had far fewer hoops to jump through. I remember that blind reverend so well. Never would that building have been saved without his faith. I can't think of a more rewarding project during that time.

After about a year of consulting with Robb & Associates, I got a phone call from Ed Dering, who had worked in the Richmond office during my time as HUD director. Before I left, he had asked me to write him a recommendation for a midcareer scholarship from HUD as he applied to Harvard's Kennedy School of Business. Upon graduating, Ed contacted me. At the end of the call, he made his pitch.

"I really enjoyed working for you," I remember him saying. "I'm interested in going into housing, and I wonder if you'd want to work together."

This was exactly the type of partnership I needed. Ed's B school training gave him a focus I didn't have. I knew how to work through bureaucracy, but he understood how to compute, which came in handy when advising clients on how big of a loan to request. About a year after filing for Robb & Associates, I changed the name of the business to Robb, Dering & Associates.

∶ 66 ∶

When Ed Dering joined me, we moved the office from Rittenhouse Square to the Bourse building in Old City. Peggy also spent some time working as a secretary for Robb, Dering & Associates and insisted that Ed refer to her as "Ms. Armstrong" on the job. Ed recently was divorced and had some extra time on his hands, so he volunteered to help us complete some home rehabilitation projects. Even though he's only about twelve years younger, he became a type of son to me.

Our different skill sets made for a fantastic partnership. Ed's ability to calculate borrowing potential and assess financial risk factors gave me more confidence to take on worthy yet complicated projects.

One of our first endeavors involved a housing need in Lebanon, Pennsylvania. A church approached us with an interest in constructing new housing for the elderly. Ed and I told them they would be better candidates for HUD approval if they formed a collective with other congregations in the area. Fortunately, they listened to this advice.

The group first focused on a wonderful isolated plot of land outside of town. I told them this wasn't a good idea. "You don't want to telegraph to your elders that you want them out of the way," I said.

Again they listened to this advice. Soon we learned there was a school building up for sale. I encouraged them to buy this property. Located in the center of activity, it would allow the seniors to engage in volunteer services with younger people at the adjoining high school. Elderly people need to be involved in civic activity with members of younger generations. It helps them feel and recognize that they are essential members of their neighborhoods.

The churches agreed with the location but the community at large did not. I'm not sure why so many were so dead set against this idea. They probably had an emotional attachment to the space, its aesthetics, and history.

Ed and I overheard various points of discussion at a Lebanon County meeting where proposals like this are adjudicated. For us, the challenge was helping the congregations understand how much money they needed to raise or borrow to afford the property and the renovations.

Time and time again, my greatest challenge has been in representing people who don't understand the dynamics of government loans. Church groups, especially, often don't have a clue of what goes into navigating bureaucratic red tape. To find a successful fit for a low-income housing application, I have to gussy something up that makes sense to a government entity. I have to present a good project that convinces the federal housing authorities that this particular low-income group will be able to reach its goals. And unfortunately, the low-income group doesn't understand that I am presenting it with the best opportunity available. Its leaders or membership sees a monetary number, often fears the amount, then starts criticizing the assessment. So often they are unaware that I'm giving them the best solution to a problem that they hired me to help them solve.

For the Lebanon project, I secured an appraiser's assessment and felt it fair and within the church consortium's budget. I knew that if they trusted me and Ed and followed our guidance, they would get the government funding they needed. When I revealed the amount at the Lebanon County meeting, whispered disagreements turned into outbursts. A lively debate followed. The loudest voice came from a "tub-thumping" minister.

Pointing at me, the man yelled, "There's only one person in the room who knows what the real value should be and it's that Philadelphia riverboat gambler!"

I kind of laughed. What do you say to something like that? Lebanon is deep in Mennonite country, and to more than a few of its religious residents, Philadelphia was just a den of sinners and fast life.

But the project succeeded as Ed and I envisioned it would. The place became a real gathering spot for the community that had fought it. One of the nice things about having multiple churches involved was the amount of support that came from so many sources. If ever there was a problem, the churches would compete to resolve it.

⁖ 67 ⁖

After several years of a very satisfying business partnership, Ed remarried and decided to move to Florida. It offered him better weather and different professional opportunities. I was on my own again with Robb & Associates.

Around the time that Ed moved south, a Yale classmate named Ken Liebman contacted me about a New York City venture. He was involved in a nonprofit called Grand Street that was interested in adding housing to their mission, and he wanted to know if I might talk with the group's director. Once again, I realized how I had undervalued what my time at HUD had meant.

I met with Grand Street's director and board and talked to them about various available government financing programs. Early on it was apparent that the NYC HUD office was willing to accept whatever plan I would help put together, so this was an exciting project from the start. After finding the right design, we settled into finding the right location. This became a cumbersome struggle that lasted for years. Rudy Giuliani was mayor of New York City then, and he essentially had locked up all development opportunities in the city that contained gardens. On the surface, this looked like an environmental effort, but really he wanted to save the properties for developers he had a special working relationship with.

We found an empty space in the Lower East Side that would have served our project wonderfully. There were no gardens there. But as soon as we made our application, someone showed up with some seeds and planted a few flowers, hoping Giuliani's watchdogs would deny our efforts. This happened again and again. It was like we were playing tag with the mayor.

Fortunately, Grand Street had a very good reputation for its nonprofit work in the Hispanic community and it found a way to leverage its influence with powers other than Giuliani's. Eventually we acquired some land and broke ground for what had become a long-awaited project. On the first day of construction, the base of the site collapsed into a sinkhole causing yet another delay. It would take about five years for Grand Street to realize this project from inception to development.

By then I had come into contact with a lawyer and real estate developer in northern New Jersey named Barry Segal. Barry encouraged me to form a nonprofit entity, which would allow me to be more competitive when bidding on projects. As a nonprofit, I could benefit from gubernatorial largesse, directing grant funds into affordable housing, as compared to for-profit developers, who would be expected to flip properties into high-end condominium living for the wealthy. Barry Segal had so many good ideas and asked so many questions that I came to value his business advice. At his suggestion, I looked for a nonprofit in New Jersey that was on its last leg, one that I could assume leadership of and repurpose for my housing agenda. Barry helped me find one called North County Conservancy. My first project with North County became a collaborative effort with Grand Street.

Once again, my name had come to Barry through the New York City HUD office. Asking about consultants, he was directed to me. I was always so impressed with Barry's vision.

He could always see ten yards ahead of everyone else. As my colleague Gary Ickowicz said, Barry Segal was a man with a great vision moving forward but a terrible rearview mirror.

At one point Barry developed a tax credit project in northern New Jersey that had been under very bad management for some time. Many tenants had made a home in the property without having to comport with federal regulations. Barry tried again and again to explain to these people that they were under new management and had to rearrange their situations within the property so that it could comply with the city code.

One man became more than a little frustrated with Barry's attempt to reassign him to a different unit for rehabilitation purposes. Barry tried to explain that he could later return to his original unit, but the man couldn't understand. He had lived there for 15 years and it seemed Barry was persecuting him. So he shot and killed Barry on the premises. It was a horrible situation and quite a horrific thing to learn about. Barry was a good man.

Gary Ickowicz, whom Barry had introduced me to, is now a partner of mine in North County Conservancy. He made a real effort to help Barry's widow financially benefit from NCC projects in development.

GRAND STREET NOT ONLY OPENED A PROFESSIONAL window for me into New York City but also refined my role as a consultant. My clientele became community-based nonprofits that were very secure and involved in most everything but housing before I encouraged them to enter that market.

ACT THREE

~⁄~

*"If we merge mercy with might, and might with right,
then love becomes our legacy and change
our children's birthright."*

—Amanda Gorman, "The Hill We Climb"

⁖ 68 ⁖

U pon graduating from Central High School, my son David chose to head to Boston University. I had entertained visions of his attending Yale. I had taken all of the children up for reunions, and they got along fabulously with my classmates, but I didn't want to force my will on the kids. I had to come to grips with the fact that had I applied to Yale in the mid-1970s, I probably wouldn't have been successful. Competition for admission just wasn't as fierce back when I had applied. Plus, it seemed none of the children were interested in going there. As much as I wanted one of them to go to Yale, I reminded myself of my relationship with my father. He had wanted me to go to Harvard, and I had found my own path. With my track record, how could I demand they do something that I had refused to do? I was the beneficiary of being able to choose, and I didn't want to narrow their options.

At the time, Boston University was one of the most expensive schools in the country. Peg and I borrowed all that we could to meet tuition. We agreed that a good education was one of the most important things we could give the kids.

As David went north, Felicia set her eyes on Washington, DC. When Georgetown entered into the conversation, Mother reminded me of something: Her grandmother Ida Barry Ryan had made a substantial donation to the school, and in doing so, established four scholarships for her heirs.

Mother remembered that her father had used one for the son of his barber. As far as any of us knew, none of the others had been claimed.

Ida Barry Ryan's support of the Catholic Church was recognized by the pope in 1907, the year Mother was born. In honor of her benevolence, Pope Pius X made her a countess of the Holy Roman Empire. Ida and Thomas Fortune Ryan invested in numerous cathedrals, including one in Richmond, Virginia, that includes a family vault. That's where Peg rests. One day I'll be interred there as well.

Ida had great respect for the Jesuit order, and her generous donation to Georgetown resulted in a building on the campus. But she must have suspected that the school might fail to honor its commitment. So on the side of the building, she had them chisel the agreement: that in recognition of her funds, the university would grant four scholarships in perpetuity for her descendants.

I took this information to the admissions officers of the school.

"I'm a descendant of Ida Barry Ryan," I said, "and I believe our family can still claim three of the four scholarships promised to us."

One man flat out said to me, "There is no record of these scholarships." The others with him balked. So I asked them to walk outside with me. Pulling back shrubbery from the engraved stone, I showed them what had been chiseled on Ryan Hall.

IDA M. RYAN HALL
ITS REVENUES PROVIDE IN PERPETUUM
FOR THE
JOHN BARRY RYAN, WILLIAM KEANE RYAN

ALLAN A. RYAN, CLENDENIN J. RYAN
JOSEPH J. RYAN
SCHOLARSHIPS.

They didn't know what to say. Other than I wouldn't be getting any kind of scholarship.

I think that as generations passed, any one of a number of Georgetown lawyers aware of the deal said, "They'll never collect on these scholarships. They have enough wealth."

I tried contacting various members of the university's board, but nobody would talk to me about this. At one point, a school officer said all of the scholarships were used up by my grandfather's barber's son; that instead of four four-year scholarships, the terms of the agreement included only four years of one scholarship.

So I found myself a Roman Catholic lawyer who practiced in DC. He licked his lips as he heard the story.

"I can't wait," he told me.

The lawyer wrote a letter to Georgetown saying if they didn't give the scholarships as promised, the Ryan family would take the building back.

It was a genius move. Mother, though, was beside herself. She had weathered so many gossip stories in so many gossip magazines about her family that she feared another round was coming.

I said the time had passed for juicy stories about the Ryans.

"What are we going to do with a building at Georgetown?" Mother asked.

The family thought I had lost my mind. But I was convinced this was the right approach. Ida Barry had given a significant financial gift and the school was acting as if it had never happened. I didn't care who found out.

The lawyer's plan worked. Georgetown awarded Felicia her scholarship.

❧ 69 ❧

eg and I eventually had three kids in college at the same time but only needed to pay two tuitions. Within a year or two of Felicia's entrance to Georgetown, Greg followed her to DC and enrolled in the journalism program at George Washington University.

From a young age, Greg has had an eye for detail and an inquiring mind. I remember his spotting things on walks, some detail on the landscape, that I never noticed. He was a young student of human behavior as well as nature. Greg had a knack for reading body language as a child and often would ask me and Peg why adults interacted the way they did. I think this is one reason why he loves traveling so much; he enjoys seeing how people operate in different landscapes and situations. Of all the children, I think Greg had the greatest appreciation for visiting Canada, seeing the old family properties, and considering the histories of the Ryans and the Robbs as rooted in Murray Bay. I enjoy going places with him now and so did Peg. Before she fell ill, Peg and Greg took a trip together in Virginia that led to their car running out of gas. That kind of memory would conjure exasperation in some mothers but Peg only spoke of it with laughter. She thought it was typical of a Greg adventure and loved it.

Greg's children, Ellie and Jeffrey, are both actors, and I'm sure they got part of their acting bug from him. I remember Greg played a part in the musical *Oliver*, and once during his Harrisburg Academy years, he took a real joy in playing the back end of a horse.

"I'm a star!" he would say.

Even that type of minor role perhaps contributed to Greg's empathy and his eye for stories. He's not a man who comes in with a thunder saying, "It's my way or the highway." He looks at the issues, considers them, and tries to understand why somebody is doing what they're doing. At GW, Greg didn't feel that the school supported this type of human-interest journalism, so he started his own paper. That didn't please the powers that be. Some administrator or other contacted us and expressed their frustration with Greg's intentions and independence. We weren't surprised. With a twinkle in his eye, he has always liked pushing the line of demarcation. I think he got that fiery spirit from me, although I'm not sure at the time that either one of us recognized how alike we are.

However, he is far more patient with me than I have been with him at times. I tried my best to be a good father, but I must say that I wasn't the most patient. Particularly when the children were small and Peg had her bout with depression, I could blow pretty quickly.

As we raised the children, I tried to connect with them in the evenings by being present at dinner, for example, and taking those wonderful evening walks around the Latham farm in central Pennsylvania. In Philadelphia, sports gave us something to rally around, and we attended many Eagles games as season ticket holders. The team wasn't so hot during many of these games in the 1970s, and it was Greg who once said to me, "Dad, I love the tickets, but did you take us here to learn to be losers?"

Now he and I share an appreciation for soccer. Ellie and Jeffrey always played in school, and Greg became involved as a referee and an avid fan of the sport. He's taught me quite a bit about the game. Just recently we were on the phone talking about an international brouhaha that threatened to reorganize the European soccer teams. I was very interested in understanding it, and Greg must have spent the better part of thirty minutes breaking the whole thing and its complicated history down for me. It was such a gift to have him take me through the situation, present both sides, and patiently listen to my repeated questions. It was more than I felt I deserved.

⁖ 70 ⁖

I can't say enough about how membership in civic and cultural groups enhances life. Whenever I've moved somewhere, I've made an effort to get involved in such organizations that contribute to my immediate neighborhood.

For a time, Peg and I became very involved in the Society Hill Civic Association, where I served as president. After leaving HUD, I became ashamed of how a lot of its financing and "urban renewal" translated into gentrification and "Black removal." In Society Hill, in particular, many longtime Black residents were forced to vacate over higher rents. When I heard that HUD was trying to start a housing project on Seventh and Pine, I became pretty excited. I saw this as a way to bring a portion of the population back that had left during my tenure.

Many of the neighbors heartily disagreed.

"There go our values!" I heard again and again.

I went to town to try to convince every naysayer that this was an important project. Many didn't listen. Aware of the neighborhood fabric, I convinced the developer early on that he needed to make an agreement with the civic association so that it could have some kind of say in management. This calmed many people down, and the project did come to fruition. I think it still falls under Section 8 housing. There is a mandate that once developers receive Section 8 funding, they must maintain the property as low-income housing for twenty years before making any adjustments. I'm pretty sure that that property still has some Section 8 tenants. And the neighborhood still has a few people who won't forgive me for "putting the community at risk."

But worried as it was, Society Hill has never needed to fret over that building's tenants. True neighbors, the tenants are some of the first to shovel and salt the sidewalks whenever snow falls. *The Philadelphia Inquirer* even awarded them a snow removal recognition.

I didn't run for reelection as president after that episode. I still contribute financially as a member, but I saw that particular involvement as a duty and nothing more.

I'VE BEEN A MUCH MORE ACTIVE MEMBER OF THE ATHenaeum, one of the first groups that Peg and I joined here in Philadelphia, located just across Washington Square from my home.

The Athenaeum of Philadelphia is a special collections library and museum that dates to 1814, a time before today's library system. To access book collections then, a person would have to go to a college or institution as books were quite expensive. Membership in a subscription library like the Athenaeum allowed people to share in that library's collection for a nominal fee. Peg and I felt it quite special to have a small library in our backyard, so we became shareholders; membership at this level allowed us to enjoy privileges such as access to special talks and events. It was definitely a neighborhood asset.

I became such a frequent user of the library that one of the librarians asked one day whether I would be interested in participating on a book nominating committee. Since

1950, the Athenaeum has given an annual literary award to an author residing in or around Philadelphia. I joined the nominating group and have received so much joy from reading books by local authors.

THE CULTURAL GROUP THAT HAS PERHAPS RECEIVED THE most of my time, treasure, and talent is the Philadelphia Society for the Preservation of Landmarks ("Landmarks"). When I first moved here in the early 1970s, I spent a lot of time with a cousin of my father's named David Robb. David had a love for historic preservation and was very involved in Landmarks. Before long, Peg and I became members as well. David and Peg hit it off because of their shared interest in family history. It was David who helped Peg nurture her interest in genealogy, and today I have a few binders of her work tracing the Ryan, Robb, and Tack families.

Joining Landmarks reinforced our investment in the neighborhood. The nonprofit was spectacularly under-funded, and it became evident right away that my primary contribution to their work needed to be fundraising. I've also made an effort to attract new donors and steer open-minded people into board positions. It can be difficult to promote forward-thinking initiatives among some historic preservationists. (I remember a fight among members who were such stuffy adherents to their interpretive visions that they argued over where the deck chairs should go on the Powel House grounds.)

I think I have a greater connection to Landmarks because of my fondness for my father's cousin, even so many years after his passing. My son, David, should certainly have a fondness for this cultural group as well.

After spending a couple of decades focused on bringing in "new blood" to Landmarks, I started pushing for a "Young Friends" group in the mid-'90s or so. When it began, I picked up the phone and called my son, David, asking him to join and encourage his friends and colleagues to do likewise. David always had a good group of friends that Peg and I enjoyed meeting.

By then David had established himself as an investment consultant, the very type of job that Bob Ellinger had so badly wanted for me. Bob couldn't have been more pleased with David's career path. The two often talked shop, and over time David benefited from Bob's business acumen. At first he had thought his grandfather had an oversimplistic approach to the stock market. Bob advocated prioritizing dividends above all else. "Always see how much the dividend is paying," Bob would say. "Don't expect stocks to pay dividends." David would nod but not really agree. And then years later, he remembered Bob's advice and noticed that he was pushing stocks that had appreciated so much that we were paying capital gains beyond the pale.

When he wasn't building his career, David played a lot of squash and also enjoyed his single blessedness. Peg and I couldn't keep up with whom he was dating. No woman could hold his interest for very long. I remember our taking David and one of his women friends to Virginia, then planning to meet them the following week for dinner after the trip. David showed up with a different woman. Peg inappropriately asked about the other woman in front of David's date, much to his embarrassment. In later years, this episode brought much amusement to the family.

David had said he would never get married. Then he connected with a woman named Elizabeth Hutchins, whom he had known for some time. Elizabeth lived nearby in Society Hill, and she was also part of the network of young professionals who supported the Young Friends chapters of various preservation, arts, and cultural groups. Soon after the two started dating, she talked him into going to Paris with her. The minute I heard about that trip, I said to Peg, "We can book the wedding." He came back head over heels for that woman, and she has been a dynamite daughter-in-law. They and their children, Caroline and Hunter, live nearby and, like me, attend Old St. Joe's Church. A nutritionist, Elizabeth has kept an eye on my diet. I've thrown dairy and most sweets out the window, and my diminished pant size has her to thank.

⁓ 71 ⁓

By the time David wed, Felicia and Greg already had spouses. Having married right after college, Greg also had two children, Jeffrey and Eleanor. Boy, did Peg and I love playing the role of doting grandparents (I still do!).

After Felicia graduated from Georgetown, she moved back to Philadelphia and lived at home while looking for a job. For some time she worked in development for the Curtis School of Music, then she headed for Boston. This move was something of a mystery to me. I knew she wasn't destined for a career in development, but she certainly could have pursued a different path while staying at home, rent-free, with a community she had cultivated over the years. Instead, she picked up and pursued a life in an entirely different city. Upon reflection, I understand her choice. She didn't want the familiar route. She wanted an adventure. It reminds me of how I turned away from Mother and Bob's expectations when I enlisted in the Navy, then later moved to Arizona. I'm proud of Felicia's grit.

In Boston, Felicia worked at a school then applied to Harvard's Graduate School of Education. For the first time since Hampton died, I had someone in my immediate family to banter with about the merits of Harvard versus Yale. It was at Harvard that Felicia met Joel Vargas. My future son-in-law impressed me from the moment I met him. There is something about his level-headed, no-nonsense, caring approach that commands respect. He even managed to earn the favor of Bob Ellinger, a stamp of approval that came easily to no man.

Felicia and Joel decided to marry in New York City. The ceremony, to my delight, was at St. Jean Baptiste's, the church built by my great-grandparents Thomas Fortune and Ida Barry Ryan, where Mal took me every Sunday as a child. The family had remained close to the priests there, and Felicia had always loved the setting. The reception was planned for the Yale Club, where our family had celebrated Thanksgiving every year with Bob for some time. For too long I had been far too cheap to get my own membership to the Yale Club, so my good friend Ed Barlow let me use his membership number. A fellow Book & Snake member, Ed was such a close friend that he had spent time with my family at Uncle Ted's Connecticut ranch back when we were students. He prided himself on supporting the Yale Club and recruiting his classmates to join, so every time I went to New York, at his encouragement I would put my tab on his account and settle up with him later.

When Felicia decided to hold her reception there, I finally ponied up and got my own membership. But at some point I had given her Ed's number, and that was the one she used to charge all of the wedding expenses. I hadn't realized the miscommunication until I got a very funny phone call from Ed one night.

"Look, Ted," he said, "We're very good friends, and I'm happy that you use the club, but my being responsible for your daughter's wedding is a bit much." To this day, we laugh and laugh about that.

The event was one of our family's most joyful occasions. Felicia was radiant, and our family gained a welcome asset in Joel—even though he later whisked our beloved girl across the country to a happy life in northern California.

⁖ 72 ⁖

B y the time Felicia and Joel married, Mother had passed away. She died in 1980, a memorable year for two very different reasons.

Mother had a slow, debilitating death. It became increasingly painful to watch her suffer from the ravages of cancer. Peg did her best to encourage me to visit the apartment on 79th Street and Lexington, but every time I did, I'd later say, "I'm beginning to forget what she looked like when she was healthy."

I just wanted to remember Mother as she was in better days. It would take me decades before I could really sit down and think about our relationship as mother and son. After Mother passed, Bob Ellinger lived another ten years or so before succumbing to dementia. I hired a live-in nurse named Julia to take care of him. In Bob's last days, a hospice nurse told me to surround him with familiar things that gave him comfort. I had pictures of Mother placed around his bed.

Bob brought Mother's life together. When they got together, he was the one who helped reorganize her life. I give him full credit for that as he took a significant feeling of responsibility for Mother's welfare off of my shoulders. Mother's various marriages had taken a toll on her bank account. She was in danger of losing all of her inheritance from Thomas Fortune Ryan. This was something that she and some of her cousins, unfortunately, had in common. For so many of that third generation, the fortune just disappeared. But Bob made a bold move in stepping in and examining her finances. She had more scattered around than she thought she did, and Bob reinvested it. This action preserved some of her inheritance for future generations.

When Mother died, I came into the trust that Bob had established. For the first time in our married lives, Peg and I didn't have to worry about money.

1980 ALSO MARKED THE YEAR WHEN I ENTERED INTO one of the most challenging and satisfying positions of my life. I joined the board of Lincoln University.

When I consider my professional and personal paths, I'm proud of the ways I had challenged myself and rebelled against the safer, more comfortable choices that Mother and Bob had wanted for me. Repeatedly I had been encouraged to pursue careers that would have given me very large bank accounts, but repeatedly I chose public service and to work for the greater good.

For a long time I thought that, for a boy raised on the Upper East Side and educated in the best schools, I had a vast knowledge of the American social record. But then I joined Lincoln's board, and I realized I didn't know the first thing about the history of Black oppression.

∻ 73 ∻

I t was Governor Dick Thornburgh who introduced me to Lincoln University, a school established in 1854 as America's first Black college. I had known Thornburgh for some time, having helped his gubernatorial campaign as a fundraiser. Soon after he took office, he approached me with a specific concern and opportunity.

"Ted, I have this appointment, and I know of few Republicans who can hack it," he said.

Each governor of Pennsylvania has the option to appoint a representative to each of the state's commonwealth campuses. Some ignore this, seeing it as an option of their service, and others, like Thornburgh, took it very seriously. Thornburgh thought it very important for a Republican governor to show interest in a Black college. But this would be a tricky appointment. He needed someone who wouldn't walk in and shoot his mouth off, trying to control the agenda. He needed someone willing to listen.

Thornburgh gave me a brief that contained a full history of the school and asked that I not decide until I had read it. I did and then accepted the appointment. The governor had no larger agenda as I wasn't even required to submit notes, and I never received a directive from his office. Every six months or so, though, I'd send a report. I think Thornburgh at the outset thought I'd serve for three years, which would take him to the end of his term and me to the natural end of a board member's service.

I've served on Lincoln's board now for forty-one years. (After seven years as an active board member, I received an honorary degree and became an emeritus trustee).

When I showed up for the first meeting in 1980, I was one of two white men at a table with twenty-five Black men. The other white man was John Ware, a former state senator whom I had worked with while serving as secretary of labor. Ware had been appointed to Lincoln by the state Senate. This choice made a lot of sense, as I remembered that he had strong minority support for his campaign. I liked Ware very much and often would seek his counsel on Lincoln politics and procedures. Boy, did I need it.

At that first meeting, I felt the pressure of a minority trustee. Unlike Ware, I had no direct tie to minority communities. I could sense the suspicious glances. Everyone there knew that I was a political appointee. They had no reason to think that I had more of an investment in helping the university.

The first item on the agenda offered me a crucial test. I'll never forget it. The board chair brought up the name of a man they were considering for an honorary doctorate, then he looked directly at me.

"For those of you who don't know," he said, then delivered an explanation of who the man was: the first Black attorney to argue a case before the Supreme Court. I had never heard of him before. After he spoke to me with a hint of a condescension, he paused. The room was silent. They clearly wanted to see if I would take offense at being singled out in this way.

I didn't miss a beat.

"Okay by me!" I proclaimed.

The whole group fell apart laughing. I know they expected me to say something like, "How dare you make me think that I don't know?"

Clearly, I passed the first test. Thornburgh had clued me in to the history of appointments, and I knew it might be a rough journey. But gradually, through meeting participation and various conversations, I made it clear that I had done some research into the school's history.

Upon my retirement from the board after seven years, just before I received the emeritus trustee distinction, one board member gave me a black wooden statue of Rodin's "The Thinker." When he presented it to me, he said, "Ted, I could see that you thought about every issue."

I could have cried. To this day, that is one of the finest gifts I have ever received.

WHAT I HAVE BEST BEEN ABLE TO HELP CULTIVATE AT Lincoln is a spirit of philanthropy. So many of the members were pastors or social service workers. For a long time, the board operated on the idea that the contribution of one's time was an in-kind donation to the school. And this is true. But I firmly believe that it is important that every member of a board contribute financially. Potential substantial donors will sometimes look to see if board members have donated their own money before they decide whether to write a check. There's a type of principle behind this that I discussed with John Ware at one point. At the time he and I were the only two members who contributed financially. When he agreed with me, I started speaking to each board member individually, saying that I believed we needed to have 100 percent of board members contributing. It did not matter one iota, I said, how much each member gave.

"We're all in," I said again and again.

It was touchy at times, but I convinced the group that this was important. And once they invested their own money, they were more inclined to ask others in their networks to do the same.

⁙ 74 ⁙

I had great hopes at one point to unite Lincoln with another great passion of mine—the Yale Class of 1956.

One of the things that makes me proudest of my class has been its development of a class treasury, for which I served as treasurer for a time. This treasury allows us to support and contribute to causes that we class members believe in. For example, we initiated a Class of 1956 scholarship fund that is awarded yearly. Our descendants qualify as potential recipients of this award, but they must apply like anyone else.

Throughout the 20th century, a large gulf developed between the city of New Haven and Yale. The university, with its substantial endowments, is one of the wealthiest in the country, and until recent years, it didn't try too hard to connect with poverty-stricken neighborhoods in New Haven. Finding a way to bridge this gap became a passion of mine and other classmates.

So we decided to join other classes to adopt a version of the "I Have A Dream Project" that originated in New York City in the early 1980s. Over 150 similar projects had since sprung up across the country, and the goal of each was to connect a wealthy entity in a poor area with the local community. For our "I Have A Dream" project, the Class of 1956 decided to "adopt" the fourth-grade class of East Rock Community School, a public school in New Haven. After securing pledges of up to $1 million, we launched a program that committed to funding the college tuition of every one of the fifty-six children in that fourth-grade class. First, though, they would have to graduate from high school, so it offered an initiative for the kids to stay in school. By the time they were juniors, thirty kids of that fourth-grade class were still enrolled in the school district.

I decided to arrange a round-trip bus tour for these high school juniors to visit Lincoln University. The kids had a ball, and the students at Lincoln loved hosting them around campus and answering their questions. I hoped that many of them would decide to apply for admission.

At least four of them did and were accepted, but not one attended. I was devastated. But I came to understand that the nature of the urban African American community kept students closer to home. This made sense to me; after all, most of Lincoln's students were local to the Philadelphia area. I wanted the kids to come to a place that had come to mean a lot to me, and that was perhaps a well-intended yet selfish motivation. In the end, the kids had a great field trip and surely learned more about attending college wherever they might have gone.

My fellow Lincoln board members very much appreciated my efforts. I think after seeing me organizing this trip to and from Connecticut, they thought, "If this white guy can bring a whole busload of people from New Haven, what the hell are we doing?" Some had never before seen themselves as hucksters of the university. This was another way that I helped in a development capacity.

My service with Lincoln has led me to ponder things I never really questioned before. It has led me to understand a little bit about being a minority myself. I think of it perhaps as a momentum swing. Before spending time talking about Black history and culture, I knew that institutions like slavery had existed, but I had never really sat down to think about how that institution was here before any other. I feel sometimes like scales have fallen from my eyes. I sure drank the white, male, patriarchal Kool-Aid for some time.

For example, the images of the police officer kneeling on George Floyd's neck in May 2020 really surprised me. It shook me. But then I talk to people who have experienced it and worse in their communities.

I've been reading books lately on racism and the Catholic Church. They've helped me see that racism has always existed in the church in a systemic form. Before, I thought a racist was someone draped in a white sheet who hung Black people from a tree. Now I realize that you can be racist by not recognizing the truth of history. It's been a late turnaround on my part, but Lincoln was my baptism into understanding the racial divide.

I fear that Black Lives Matter doesn't resonate enough here in Philadelphia. We haven't gotten to the point where we've committed enough to moving forward. I don't think people understand the movement. They see "BLM" as a slogan but should take it more seriously. The truly marginalized communities of Philadelphia are just not "seen" by people in public conversations. Those of us who have functioned as city leaders and participated in these talks have lived in a type of impoundment. And we haven't been anxious enough to go over and see what is on the other side.

This is one reason why I'm involved in the "1619 Project." It's an effort on the part of *The New York Times* and other outlets to tell stories about the history of slavery that have been overlooked or misunderstood. I've found that learning these stories and communicating them to others is one way I can engage in the conversations that I used to fear having. I don't have political connections anymore, but I can surely acknowledge to my friends and family where I have remained silent when I could have spoken. I and my like-minded peers can share our errors with younger generations so they can do better than we have done. And if we don't think they will listen, we can invest our dollars in their causes. Then they'll have to listen.

Oh, what Bob Ellinger and Mother would have said about all of this. I look at my grandchildren Hunter and Caroline—David and Elizabeth's children, in fifth and seventh grade—and I remember that my own children were about their ages when Peg and I decided to move the family to Philadelphia. And while that decision called Mother and Bob to fear for all of our lives, I couldn't be happier that my own grandchildren are growing up in this city, witness to these times, and not merely hearing watered-down versions of civil unrest inside the confines of an Upper East Side domicile.

I couldn't be prouder of these two young people. They hear what people think, and they have the firsthand experience to draw their own ideas and conclusions. They aren't totally controlled human beings as I was at their ages. Both are so much smarter, and savvier, than I. It amazes me how Hunter can pick up and play soccer with young men from all different backgrounds. That teaches him so much about being part of a larger community that doesn't look like he does. And Caroline has such a keen eye for detail. She is a passionate artist, and I can't wait to see how her portfolio reflects her impressions of this world.

❖ 75 ❖

There have been a number of times in my life when I've questioned why God allows certain things to happen. The presidency of Donald J. Trump qualifies as one of them. I think the man is clinically nuts. I really do.

People who comport themselves like Trump have no God. I like to see my president setting a tone. When Nixon was president, telling lies in the Oval Office was a god-awful thing. Now it's par for the course. All we get out of Trump are lies and accusations. As I write this chapter, the 2020 election looms large. What the country needs is a president who doesn't rule by Twitter. I think Joe Biden would be a wonderful president. It would take him four years to undo what Trump did and settle the country down. He'd be a caretaker. It's like he'd get behind the wheel and push the brakes before the country goes over a cliff. Then he'd back it up a bit and gradually bring it back down the road so we can figure out where to go next. Meanwhile, the Republicans need to pick themselves up off the floor and figure out how to think and act positively.

They will surely need someone who will challenge Kamala Harris the next time around. To me, Kamala Harris is breathtaking. She is crackerjack smart and gets right to the point. We need her directness. That's why President Obama captivated so many people. He seemed to cut to the chase and didn't bother with inanities. His stature, his presence, and his understanding of the Constitution as a constitutional law expert made the country proud at home and overseas.

I do attribute some of today's racism to Obama's election. It unleashed extremists. But Trump allowed their aggrandizing. Now we need someone to lay down the law and directly confront the nation's problems. I'd love Biden to strip off his jacket so everyone could see his Superman shirt. He has common sense. But common sense is not something that turns the masses on.

We never see the real person who holds the office of president. So much of the presidency and what we make of it is an image. We make images of people. Now Donald Trump has created his own image, then he resents the way people interpret it and blames the media for what it says about that very image.

I'm guilty of becoming attracted to a candidate because of the image in front of me and what I perceive that image to be. And I've always judged candidates on the images of their predecessors. My voting record offers plenty of examples of this, starting with the first time I voted Democrat after campaigning for a Republican. I wasn't crazy about Lyndon Johnson in 1964, but I sure as hell wasn't going to vote for the image Barry Goldwater represented after attending the Republican Convention for that election.

Four years later, when Vice President Adlai Stevenson ran in 1968, I voted for Richard Nixon. I had spent a lot of time talking about Nixon while campaigning for Eisenhower in 1956, and by the time he had a shot at the White House, he seemed the most "presidential" option. Adlai Stevenson struck me as too hungry for power.

I voted for Gerald Ford in 1976 because I liked him very much, and I thought he helped restore normalcy to the party after Nixon's fall. Plus, Ford was easier to take than Nixon. Jimmy Carter beat him, but I didn't mind Carter. Since his term, he has become the most noble image of a former American president, and I couldn't admire him more.

I supported Carter like hell in 1980, when the California cowboy ran for office. Ronald Reagan's movie star image was just too much to take. He was very conservative and in that way reminded me of Goldwater. Reagan didn't seem to have any depth, and the 1980 election marked the second time I voted for a Democrat. But, unfortunately, Reagan won. And that was a type of death for government-supported housing. Throughout the 1980s public housing became less of a federal priority and more of a problem that people couldn't figure out. I voted for Walter Mondale in 1984 for exactly this reason.

I returned to the party to vote for George H.W. Bush in 1988. My Yale ties made it easier for me to have faith in a Republican, and it seemed he might return the party to more moderate times. I think he did, and I voted for him against Bill Clinton in 1992. But then I did become a Clinton fan. His charisma and self-confidence earned my vote in 1996, and I think he was a very good president.

It's a shame that Al Gore didn't win in 2000. George W. Bush was a Yale graduate, yes, but I was never a fan. Under his direction, the party returned to its negative days. Like Ronald Reagan, he was more pizazz and pyrotechnics than substance. I hated Bush's catchphrase of "weapons of mass destruction" as a reason for going after Saddam Hussein and the Middle East. It was too much. I could sense the political errors he would make as that motto spread like wildfire throughout the country. The Bush administration's understanding of Middle Eastern history and policies seemed wrong and filled with oversimplifications. I had traveled extensively through that part of the world and Bush's indemnification of its cultural capitals was insulting.

I was sorry to see John Kerry lose in 2004. It was interesting at the time to think of Theresa Heinz Kerry, widow of my old friend John Heinz, as First Lady. She was never warm and friendly (John Heinz died in a plane crash after a visit to Philadelphia in 1991), but I think her second husband, the senator from Massachusetts, would have made a good president.

Barack Obama captured my American spirit from the very beginning. As I mentioned before, he had a candor and rhetoric that inspired voters. I think he was a very good president because he promoted hope to parts of America that had long gone ignored. I sense Kamala Harris will one day be a worthy successor of his. And although Obama supported Hillary Clinton as his successor, she never appealed to me as a strong presidential candidate. I know that doesn't make me look very good to feminists, but I had a feeling that she was just going to mark time and not do the country much good. To me, Hillary Clinton was to the left what Trump is to the right. She treated Bernie Sanders horribly, and as much as I disliked Trump, I hated that she called his voters "deplorables." You just don't use that word to refer to people who disagree with your agenda. Still, I held my nose and voted for her in 2016.

But the most exciting recent candidate for office has been Bernie Sanders. This has made me a hero to my grandchildren and a nut to my children. Sure his platform for universal health care was and is idealistic. But too many people in America are marginalized. Health care is a basic need and right. No democracy should deny its people health care.

Sanders also has encouraged me to recognize more and more of the flaws implicit in the two-party system that has controlled America for so long. The moderate truly has died in this country, and that's not a good thing. We need a third party to grasp that moderate vote.

I'm a registered Democrat but a moderate at heart. When the moderates lost ground to extremists, that's when all the foolishness started. This is one reason why I've spent an increasing amount of time talking to Philadelphia Independents, an interesting group of all shapes, sizes, ages, makeups, and beliefs. I've had lots of fun engaging in meaningful conversations with them, in person, and now virtually during COVID-19.

One thing that Independents in Pennsylvania are pushing for is the open primary. Pennsylvania is a state that only allows Republicans or Democrats to vote in primaries, which doesn't strike me as the democratic ideal. Disliking the idea of two political parties, Independents have tackled a practical, tangible goal in trying to get open primaries in every state. Their next step will be to find a leader to rally behind. This person will need to attract more independent thinkers who refuse to slavishly follow traditional party lines. I'm fed up with both sides.

Mitch McConnell and Nancy Pelosi drive me equally nuts. McConnell is a moral failure. He's worse than Trump on one level because he truly knows right from wrong. For him, the party comes first and the country second. And Nancy Pelosi doesn't practice gentility. She thinks the party can only play hardball, and sometimes softball is the better game.

I have to think that Peg and I would be more aligned politically now in the Trump era. He has done so much damage. But, boy she and I would get into some spectacular political discussions. She was a die-hard Republican through and through.

⁙ 76 ⁙

It is sometimes strange to think that Peggy and I met through politics. I think one reason she became a staunch Republican is her aunt and uncle's household. Raised as a Democrat in her formative years, she wanted to make her own way as soon as she left their house. But Catholicism was the larger reason for her political views. It's interesting how we judge people's political beliefs by what we know of their religion. I hope this may not be so much the case in the future.

It's also ironic that Peggy, in a way, introduced me to Philadelphia Independents, which has captured so much of my political ideology. Several years before she died in 2012, Peggy had become involved in a group called Good Shepherd, a nonprofit that helps incarcerated juveniles find adult mentors who will look out for their best interests. Peggy loved her collaborations in this group. I know she felt her biological parents were missing in action in regard to her two older brothers, and that one reason they became so troubled was a lack of sound adult supervision. Good Shepherd offered Peggy a way to connect with adolescents like her brothers.

Through Good Shepherd, Peg had a list of troubled youth, and she would show up at police stations to sit with her charges and propose community-based service alternatives to jail sentences as part of negotiations with the district attorney's office. She loved this work.

Some of her youth would finish their time in the legal system and move on to productive things. Others would fall off and get arrested again, and she always took these situations as personal losses. I'd say she spent four or five years with Good Shepherd. It was someone from this group who contacted me after her death and invited me to a Philadelphia Independents meeting.

One might think that someone with such involvement in social justice might lean to the left politically. Not Peg. She really was a one-issue voter. To her, abortion was the great sin, and no political agenda would sway her from voting for an anti-abortion candidate.

I'm personally anti-abortion, but I don't think it's right to say, "If you are not pro-life, you are not Catholic." Some people just can't parent the way a child needs them to parent. If a child doesn't have nourishment or other basic needs met, what kind of life is he or she facing? Many Catholics voted for Trump just because his campaign claimed it was anti-abortion. Something is missing here. The same argument applies to LGBTQ rights.

Since joining Old St. Joe's, I've made connections with more LGBTQ people than ever before. I've seen committed LGBTQ couples with such a great love for each other that it has changed my thoughts on marriage only being for a man and a woman. When you hear personal stories and see why people make the choices they do and how they honor personal commitments, how can you say what is definitively right and wrong for a person? I don't think I'll ever see myself associated with a man sexually, but I can appreciate that all humans have different beliefs and thoughts. I can't say, "You must see the world as I see it."

My Catholic beliefs are very important to me. The Jesuits have become particularly strong in my life because I've learned that their practices and homilies make you think about what and why you believe. They don't want you to just punch in your ballot, so to speak, because you think there has to be only one right answer or candidate.

Religion gives me a community to participate in and worship with. It gives me a group to share my life with. It has strengthened my awareness of what the world is all about and what my life is all about. If I had no religion, I couldn't imagine where I might be. I'd be unhinged. It's an anchor that has given my life real meaning.

I dislike Catholics who erect doors and walls that force people to go one way down a particular hall. I remember going to Masses as a child where the priests faced away from parishioners. This practice dictated religion and told people "this is the way." In retrospect, I think Peg and I pushed this type of Catholicism onto our children too much. Each had negative reactions to some of the tenets of the church and peeled away as a result. David returned to the church after a while. Felicia got angry with it and rightly so. I don't blame her. Greg also left, but it's given me joy to see him become a Quaker and search for his own truth.

Before Peg and I attended Old St. Joe's, we attended Old St. Mary's with the family. We did it to support the parish connected to the school the children attended when we first moved to Philadelphia. It wasn't a good choice for a church. I remember the priest at the time was truly a drunkard. Peg so wanted the boys to be part of the Mass as servers, and when I asked the priest about this, he said they didn't have any vestments. I asked how hard it would be to get some. They finally arrived and the boys served as altar boys to make their mother happy.

When Peg and I decided to move on to Old St. Joe's, I found such a home with the Jesuits. So did she. In fact, before we left Old St. Mary's, Peg attended Masses at both churches. I never would have gone to Old St. Joe's had Peg not led that charge, and I'm so thankful she did. It has played such a key role in my life. I love how the priests there encourage parishioner involvement in Mass and parish councils, making religion so much more accessible.

I believe that when I pass away, I'll be able to get to heaven. I have faith that I'll run into Peg there.

❧ 77 ❧

I think a lot about legacies these days.

For the past few years, I've served as the secretary for my Yale class of 1956, which means that every other month I submit a column to the alumni magazine. When any of our classmates dies, my column includes an obituary. The number of words I am allotted depends on the number of surviving class members.

When I hear of someone's passing, I'll get in touch with a family member and an alumni friend or two if possible. I look forward to these interactions because, in addition to including the obvious details (survivors, occupation, cause of death), I am passionate about locating stories and memories that will allow me to show how this person made the world a better place. So I focus on what 1956 graduates contributed to their communities, rather than their business accomplishments. Sometimes people don't like this approach.

For example, not too long ago, we lost a classmate who had made a name for himself in industry and had become a vocal right-wing supporter. I got about a dozen letters from individuals in various classes saying I didn't give him his proper due. More than one said I was a spokesperson for a "leftist Yale organization." What I try to tell these critics in so many words is that I see it as my job to uphold the motto established by our class during its 10th reunion: "Friendship Lasts." More than serving a political agenda or listing everything on a resumé, I want to do my best to show how this person was there for other people.

Being class secretary also affords me the opportunity to help plan our five-year class reunions. I don't think I've missed one since I graduated in 1956.

When it comes time for someone to write my obituary, I hope I will be remembered as a good husband, father, and grandfather. I'm blessed to have been able to apply my time, talent, and treasure to worthwhile civic associations, and I know I'll be noted for my work as secretary of labor and regional director of HUD. I've had the good fortune to meet a lot of interesting people, though not all of them will be considered interesting by the outside world. People like to hear stories filled with names like Nixon and Ford, Rizzo and Romney, but the project that has meant the most to me doesn't have recognizable names attached to it. I'm glad that I embarked upon it before Peg died so she could learn a little bit about the signature work that I would choose to mark my legacy.

⁖ 78 ⁖

In the early 2000s, I was contacted by state Representative Marie Lederer. She had learned that Temple University was soon to sell Neumann Medical Center in Fishtown, a neighborhood within her district. She feared the historic buildings would fall into the hands of a greedy developer who would raze and replace them with "luxury condos."

Temple had taken charge of Neumann Medical Center in the 1970s. The site had first hosted a hospital over 100 years before, when the Sisters of St. Francis founded it as St. Mary's Hospital just before the Civil War began. St. Mary's began in a townhouse-size building in 1860. Back then, before ambulances, horse teams brought the sick and wounded (often from local factories) to St. Mary's, where the largely immigrant community received free health care.

The property grew, and when St. Mary's found a larger home north of the city in Bucks County, the hospital here was renamed St. Neumann's. While I didn't think of it at the time, I now know that my grandfather Hunter Robb spent his early career in Kensington, the larger neighborhood that encompasses Fishtown. His work, on occasion, must have taken him a half-mile from the Kensington Hospital for Women to what was then called St. Mary's.

After my phone call with Marie Lederer, I learned that the buildings in question dated to 1898 and 1915 and included about 70,000 square feet. I was very hesitant to take on the project, especially after I visited. As I suspected, the building's architecture was absolutely beautiful. To convert it into low-income housing would cost a fortune. This would be the largest project I had overseen, and I knew that HUD probably would allow only ninety-six dollars per square foot of reconstruction (at best). This was less than half the amount that contractors would want.

Nevertheless, I contacted architect Cecil Baker, a veteran of HUD work whom I had worked with before. He and I spent two nights in sleeping bags camping out in the old abandoned hospital as we thought about what we could do. It was kind of eerie.

The property is a historic preservationist's dream. Cast-iron balustrades decorate columned porches that reach four stories high. Most of the exterior materials—brick, limestone, granite, and terracotta—needed restoration. Inside, painted murals decorate the walls, beautifully complementing stained-glass illustrations that pop up everywhere. In addition to two elevators, a restored grand staircase connects the building's five floors. Most rooms feature 10-foot-tall ceilings, many have floor-to-ceiling bay windows, and quite a few have roof terraces. Interior units look down on a lovely private courtyard. The property's crown jewel, though, is a domed chapel decorated with ornate stained-glass windows.

After my initial hesitation, I fell in love with the building. Cecil and I envisioned that it could hold sixty-nine one-bedroom units for low-income senior citizens. We planned for a large community room on the third floor, and Cecil designed each of the residential floors to have its own lounge and living room area. All of these things eventually came to fruition. But for it to succeed, I had to use every part of my professional reputation and call upon every option I had learned about navigating low-income housing applications.

For North County Conservancy to make good on its end of the deal with Temple University, the project had to survive three main challenges: a fire caused by a welding spark, a constant stream of structural problems, and an obscene amount of funding paperwork. Had I not had my experience as HUD director, I don't know how we would have found our way through all of the red tape we had to break. For example, I knew that the Catholic chapel would require a good amount of work, and I also knew the government would not permit me to fund any religious portion of the project. So I kept that out of the application, knowing we could find a way to ethically include that in later stages of the work.

Tenacity and savvy allowed us to secure a HUD mortgage of $10 million, $1 million from the city of Philadelphia, and $400,000 from the state of Pennsylvania. To qualify for residency, seniors must have a maximum fixed income of $24,000. They then pay 30 percent of their adjusted gross income in rent (heat and water are included). The waiting list is quite long.

Nearly seventeen years after work began in 2004, it is a true joy for me to walk around Neumann Senior Housing, especially when I'm feeling low. The chapel brings me such serenity. Before the pandemic, I took prayers and conversations with my guardian angel there. And how I have always loved talking to the tenants. The connections they have to the building are something else—more than a few were even born there. One woman's apartment is in a former waiting room where she once sat during an operation for one of her children.

These conversations and connections remind me of what life is all about: creating safe spaces for people to grow and share their stories. Now during the pandemic, I can only hope that the tenants find ways to continue to talk to one another about their memories. Fortitude comes from owning and voicing one's past, and hope comes from hearing the survival stories of others.

⁖ 79 ⁖

That being said, an enjoyable companion during this time of isolation has been TMC, the Turner Movie Classics network. Peg and I used to go to the movies often enough, but watching films on my own had never been much of a hobby before now. How I have loved tuning in to TMC as the primetime host Ben Mankiewicz shares "behind the scenes" tales and critics' takes of classic films like *Gone with the Wind* and more contemporary movies like *Nebraska*. I have found myself in tears more than once while considering the stories I've heard of misunderstood talent, transient fame, and the sheer effort it takes to get projects from scripts to screen. My favorite work so far has been one now considered a cult hit, the 1990 film *Metropolitan*. Mankiewicz categorizes the independent movie as a type of romantic dramedy, and if I were just to know the film according to its genre, I wouldn't have touched it. But it is more than terrific.

If somebody were to have satirized my young adult life, he could have put me inside of *Metropolitan*. The film takes the viewer into bourgeoise New York City society, and although it isn't exactly a period piece, it provides a timeless look at Upper East Side teenagers and their activities and conversations during the holidays—all dressed up with only the same places to go, year after year. Their cards are full of coming out parties, and they speak of who is and isn't coming, and who will be coming whether or not they were actually invited. That would have been me. As a teenager, I'd hear about a coming out party, and if Mother hadn't secured my invitation, I had a million ways of talking my way into anywhere.

The dialogue in this movie was spot-on. It offers flashes into life as I knew it exactly. I remember one character who would spout off names and titles as if he were the world's classic know-it-all. Constantly providing misinformation as truth, he was one of any number of friends I had. There also was a creator of stories that were outrageous, and an outsider who followed one path until she met a man at an eastern school and almost married him until the forces that be threw the whole thing off. I can't explain how uncanny watching that film at age 86 felt. At one point I said to myself, "I could close my eyes and appear at the door at age 16, another character at the party."

⁏ 80 ⁏

I did find a way to finally get Peg back to New York City living. In the mid- to late-1990s, she finally had the chance to pursue an acting career. Her time at Goddard, spent with so many young artists from the New York City area, had either started or encouraged this interest, and about twenty years after her graduation, she had the opportunity to secure an agent. She had the most success finding jobs as a model for advertisements. Once, as I walked down a Philadelphia street, I noticed an enormous picture of Peg arm-in-arm with a dashing man. It was an advertisement for a retirement community on the side of a SEPTA bus.

She took great pleasure in these jobs, and in between assignments, she volunteered, often spending time with the Good Shepherd program. Her auditions took her to New York City often, and how she loved that. It brings me such joy to know that our grandchildren Jeffrey and Ellie, both actors living in New York, witnessed this part of Peg's life and enjoyed moments of it with her.

New York offered a type of magic pill to Peg. Sometimes, if I could tell she was having a bad day or frustrated over something, I would encourage her to go to New York for the day. That was a cure-all. She'd take the train up in the morning, visit with friends, and come home a happy person.

The commute on a daily basis however can be quite taxing, and during a particularly fertile working period of hers, I suggested we think about securing a small apartment in Manhattan. When Jeffrey and Ellie were young, we had done this in Washington, DC, so we could keep in closer touch with the grandchildren.

One evening Peg and I talked about finding a Manhattan apartment, and by 10:30 the next morning she found one. We had a little place on East 57th Street for several years. I'd go with her sometimes to catch dinner and a show, but the apartment was so tiny it barely fit both of us at the same time. She loved it. I was so happy to be able to do that for her before her health began to unravel.

Peg developed a case of emphysema, worsened by a bout with pneumonia. She couldn't kick the pneumonia, and I think she had it for about two years. This led to multiple problems that required multiple doctors. Appointments and prescriptions became so confusing that I hired a service called "MD VIP," which gave us access to a personal physician at any time of day or night. This doctor also functions as a type of contractor that facilitates conversations between specialists. Life became a real struggle during this time. I didn't know what to do. We didn't talk much about her illness, and this was hard, especially as doctors increasingly began telling us that her symptoms would only worsen. Independent woman that she was, Peg hated having to rely on others so much.

As the years passed, I became concerned about the physical restrictions of our house and the social isolation Peg was experiencing. I thought (and many suggested) that we might benefit from moving to a place like Hopkinson House, just across the park from our house. Our house on Seventh Street doesn't have a bathroom on the first floor, so Peg had to get up and down a staircase to move between our living area, bedroom, and bath. She didn't want to think about moving from our home though, and as long as she could get through the front door and up the stairs, I thought okay. I was happy to stay in this house, familiar and comfortable for us both.

Around this time I learned of a wonderful organization called Penn's Village, in which I have since become very involved. Penn's Village has a mission to help elderly people stay in their homes as long as possible. It provides member volunteers to take people to appointments, function as advocates if need be, and offer company at home. Thinking Penn's Village would be a wonderful addition to Peg's life, I set up an interview with one of its workers at our house. I didn't tell Peg my intentions in advance.

This poor woman came to talk to us one afternoon, and about halfway into her presentation, Peg caught on. She stood up and stomped out of the room. I looked at the woman and apologized. Then I chuckled to myself. Peg still had me guessing, even after over fifty years of marriage. But I was disappointed that she didn't want to join Penn's Village. I really believe in their mission and the work they do.

There was a woman whom Peg would occasionally walk with around Washington Square, and the children did call, so Peg did speak with people. But I wanted greater social engagement for her. At night we would watch television together, yet I couldn't get her to open up about how she felt. It was reminiscent of those days long ago when the children were tiny and I feared Peg's one-word responses.

No doctor would say, "Watch out. The end is coming." That's not what they do. But by saying that things would only get worse, they were trying to prepare us. I know I was somewhat in denial, believing the old saying, "Where there's a will, there's a way." I prayed all of the time that she would get better. Every week I lit a candle for her at Old St. Joe's.

One day Peg refused to get out of bed. So I called 911, and a team of firefighters came to the house.

"I can't get her up," I said at the door.

One hunky fireman walked upstairs and lifted her from the bed. I'll never forget how she batted her eyes at him. She went to the emergency room a block away and soon felt much better. She could walk fine that evening.

But two days later she fell in the bathroom and hit her head badly. I called 911 and the same group arrived. They got her to Jefferson Hospital once again, but this time Peg never recovered. She was in a coma. I immediately contacted the kids and they came as soon as they could. We talked about our options, then I made what seemed the clear decision.

"We're kidding ourselves to keep her alive this way," I told them and myself.

I had had a difficult time getting our parish priest to visit Peg while she was failing and still at home. I thought it would be a very good idea for him to visit. After all, Father Jim's visit to Pittsburgh did her so much good all those years before. It was disappointing that our priest now didn't visit the house to offer counsel but he did visit the hospital to perform last rites. I was very appreciative of that.

Peg died at age eighty-two.

The kids sent emails all over inviting people to the funeral at Old St Joe's. And they came from all over to attend the service. Our house was packed to the brim that week. As a taxi dropped off a friend of ours at the church for the funeral, the driver asked, "Who died?" He assumed it was a dignitary or a celebrity because of the crowds.

⁚ 81 ⁚

What I remember most from Peg's memorial service is the speech given by our granddaughter Ellie. She was in high school at the time her grandmother died and would soon be entering Bard College. In so many ways it is the narrative that Peg never wrote for herself. Hearing it took my breath away. I include it here, with Ellie's permission, so that Peg's story can live alongside mine.

Margaret Armstrong Robb
By Eleanor Parker Robb

There are many ways I could remember my grandmother, Margaret Armstrong Robb. She was a part of all our lives in many ways. She was a spectacular person. Truly unique, she had grace and a presence wherever she went. Out of all the many capacities and roles she had, in my life she played three key parts: a supporter, a leader, and a teacher.

Granny always had knitting needles in her hands, crafting scarves, sweaters for friends and family. Just yesterday I learned one of my closest friends still wears the scarf Granny made her in elementary school. After the many gifts of sweaters, scarves, and hats made by Granny, I endeavored to learn how to knit like her. She taught me one summer, helping me pick yarn and giving me a pair of her needles that would do the trick. Although I learned how to knit, how she produced so many beautiful pieces is beyond me. Although I haven't figured out how to make a sweater…or a blanket…one lesson with Granny has kept me knitting throughout my life.

Granny had a way of supporting everyone around her. It is my belief she has at least one friend in every state. Not only did she keep friends by calling, visiting, mailing newspaper articles she thought they would enjoy, Granny kept them all very close. I'm sure many of you here today felt as if she always was there for you. As her grandchild, I knew Granny liked to visit and also introduce me to her friends. She also made friends wherever she went. There are countless stories to her becoming friends with Starbucks baristas as well as Amtrak conductors. One time, the two of us went into New York City to see the musical *Little Women*. As we arrived at the theater Granny realized she had forgotten the tickets back in Philadelphia. But Granny, determined that we would see the musical, became friends with people in the box office, and they led us to our seats in the front row and gave me an original cast-signed program. To this day I have no actual idea how we ended up in the best seats and given a program…

Granny led by example. She delved into family history, discovering connections and lineage that had not been explored. All of the work she did inspired me to take a greater interest in research, as well as my family history. Her passion for genealogy as well as acting reminds me of the effort and the drive I put into all of my work and activities.

Granny loved Grandparents' Day at my school. Her passion for learning influenced me as well as my classmates. Granny impressed both my Trigonometry class and Advanced Placement US History classes by participating and answering the questions correctly. But what made Granny's visit so special was the letter she sent to the school, commending the teacher and the students for the knowledge that they had that was shared with her. To this day, that letter is hanging up on a bulletin board in the offices of my school. She knew how to treat everyone she met benevolently and compassionately. Everyone loved her. And she truly loved everyone.

The roles my grandmother had in my life extend so much farther and broader than what I have said today. I am truly blessed to have had Granny as my dear friend for so many years. The traditions of changing seats throughout Thanksgiving I hope will stay in her honor. I will treasure the many things she has given me. The loss of her presence in my life, and all of yours, will be unbearable. But if my grandmother taught me anything, it would be to be strong, to support and care for everyone around you and lead on.

Well said, dear Ellie.

AS GRANDPARENTS, PEG AND I SURE INDULGED OUR SILlier sides. When Jeffrey and Ellie were little, I established a routine where I would point at an animal in a book and refer to it with the sound of another animal. "That says woof!" I would say, pointing to a cat. Oh, how they would laugh and laugh. Or I would shake their hands and smile, telling them it was time to let go when I was the one with the firmer grasp. From a young age, they nicknamed me "Silly Granddaddy," and the name, or its beloved "SG" abbreviation, sticks today.

Peg and I would have them come to Philadelphia for a weekend or week when they could, and Peg made sure they never knew exactly what to expect when they arrived. Sure they knew about the game room, and the spots in our old home that reminded them of the *Narnia* stories, such as the crawl space that links two of the rooms on the second floor. They knew they could always talk us into a trip to Jamba Juice, but they could never anticipate what Peg had in store for them. When they were ages ten and twelve, she surprised them with a trip to a homicide trial. Peg had some connection to the judge and had secured approval for the kids' attendance. They loved calling home later that evening and telling their mother where they had been.

It is the honor of a lifetime to be the grandfather of Jeffrey and Ellie, Caroline and Hunter, and the father of David, Felicia, and Greg. One reason I am writing this book is to put my life experiences in their hands. I wish I could live to read the ones they may one day write for themselves.

⁃ 82 ⁃

Felicia was the last to leave in the days after the funeral. She had worried over me, laying out my clothes, cleaning out my closet, and making sure I had meals set up. When she left, I experienced a depth of sadness I have never felt before.

I had come up with a plan to get through the first wave of grief. I was going to go down to the basement and get as many books as I could find and just stay in the house for a while and read. So I started to do that. I set up a stack of books in the living room and then sat there, feeling so horribly sad.

I clearly remember saying to myself, "I'm just going to wall off the world and let it go by."

An apparition visited me immediately.

As I started reading my second book, it was as if Peg were in the house. I envisioned her in the kitchen and myself in the living room, and we were in the middle of a conversation between the two rooms like we used to have.

It was as if I saw her crossing the threshold, and she was coming into the room to argue about what I had just said about the world passing me by. In the vision, she made it clear to me that this was not how she wanted her memory to impact my future. She didn't want her departure to be a reason for my shutting off the world.

So I decided to go to Siberia.

It took me about a year to orient myself in the house without Peg. I moved through the motions of life, but I was down in the dumps and ashamed of how low I had sunk. I knew I needed to do something to shock myself back to life.

I don't know where I saw it, but somewhere I came across an advertisement for a tour through Siberia on the Trans-Siberian Express aboard the historic Golden Eagle train. I had always loved trains.

"This is the thing I ought to do!" I thought to myself almost as soon as I saw it. I sent off for a catalog and soon told my kids I was heading to Russia.

They thought I was crazy.

I knew I had to do something. It wasn't existential questions that I had become lost in. It was nostalgia. Longing to return to days that had passed, I didn't know how to move forward. Peg was the engine that powered our coach. She was the one always finding things out and turning over rocks and saying I should look at this or look at that. And now she was gone, and I didn't know where to look. Somehow I knew that I would find what I needed in Siberia.

THE BRITISH-RUN TOUR COMPANY MADE SOME VERY helpful recommendations as I decided which tour to take. I knew I wanted to take one of the two-week trips, but I wasn't sure whether to travel east to west or west to east between Moscow and Vladivostok in the Russian Far East. Accounting for the time zone changes, the company recommended that travelers book trips going from west to east (the train moves through four different time zones). So I would fly into Moscow and then take a Russian airline to Vladivostok. There I would meet my fellow travelers aboard the Golden Express, and we would follow the historic railroad back to Moscow.

The guides also noted that most people traveled as couples and booked a shared compartment. As these rooms were much more spacious than the singles, they recommended I consider booking the double.

"If there's a nice Russian lady around who can join me, sure!" I joked. I took their advice and was glad I did.

I looked forward to meeting my traveling companions in Vladivostok with some trepidation. We would be living with one another in small quarters for fifteen days. That would feel like a very long time if the group didn't meld well. This was, after all, no trip to the Jersey shore.

I had invested a lot of money in this adventure and surely didn't want to come back with my hat in my hand.

"What if this turns out to be a real disaster?" I asked myself more than once.

Our first meeting set me at ease. I found myself amid international kindred spirits, half of whom were Australian. Their quick wit and wanderlust reminded me so much of Kevin Luscombe, my old friend from my Heinz years in Pittsburgh. There was another party from Turkey including a man from the Philadelphia suburbs. All, like me, were train enthusiasts, and we represented a nice age range.

Life aboard the train between various cultural stops included meals prepared by a private chef, lectures by a professor of Russian history, and even private concerts. One of my fondest memories was an evening spent drinking Russian beer in the bar car and singing folk songs as the train piped along. The Russian I learned in naval intelligence school sure came in handy some five decades later. I found that with a little brushing up, I could recall enough to make myself proud.

Traveling through Mongolia we stopped at various military attractions previously closed to westerners. We also visited Buddhist temples and took in a traditional Mongolian folk performance.

When I had traveled through western Russia after Yale, I had felt a hankering to go farther east beyond Moscow's boundaries. Five decades later, I now had that chance. We encountered several people who had lived in Siberia during World War II, and I strongly sensed their disillusionment. Siberia had been a type of dumping ground for iconoclasts, dissidents, and criminals even before the years of World War II and Stalin. The Trans-Siberian Express railroad had, after all, been constructed to send prisoners to a godforsaken fate of hard labor in the middle of the wilderness.

Had I encountered these individuals on my first trip, I expect they would have feared expressing their true thoughts. Not this time. They talked not about the suffering they endured, as one might expect, but their utter disrespect for the government. There was a stoic quality to their speech. They had a grudging acceptance of the cards life had dealt them, and their candor reflected the extent to which the people had challenged the state's control.

At one point, I said to myself, "You know, if I were younger and wanted to do something totally different, I'd go to Siberia and take on a business challenge." Because a deep freeze covers the land for five months a year, its agricultural richness is largely untapped. It would take a heavy investment, but a sound infrastructure would yield innumerable returns. I don't know why this part of the world has remained frozen in time. Generation after generation of monarchies and dictators prioritized Siberia's role as a prison as opposed to its wealth of natural resources. Perhaps it has been ignored so long because it holds so many stories that so many want silenced. The Russian government is consumed with control, and control freaks aren't the kind of people looking to break barriers.

This is the type of thinking that my fellow travelers and I would process at night, traveling through the dark wilderness in our cozy bar car. When I was a younger man on my voyages, I'd have these types of discussions with myself in my letters to Mother. Now I didn't have an audience waiting at home for my thoughts, and it was only instinctual to want to share new experiences. Fortunately, I had several Australians, some Turks, and a handful of Americans happy to engage. This company at this time made me feel very lucky. It gave me such gratitude for my life.

⋰ 83 ⋱

As we approached the continental divide between Asia and Europe, we made what would perhaps be the most memorable stop, to Lake Baikal, the largest freshwater lake in the entire world. The Lake Baikal region hosts one of the most pristine, crystal-clear settings I have laid eyes on in all of my travels. Because it holds few mineral salts and is frozen for six months every year, the lake is luminescent.

As the train wound through tunnels and cliffs, a voice announced through the sound system in our compartments that if we brought swimming gear, now was the time to put it on. I had come with swim trunks, as had two or three others in our group of two dozen.

We disembarked on the shoreline and a small boat took us swimmers to a float about 200 yards away. Then our guides told us that they hadn't mentioned how cold the water would be. I realized that this "swim" as they referenced it was actually an initiation into the Siberian Polar Bear Club. For a minute I felt I had been conned into doing something I had no business doing. There was a chill in the air, but the scenery had somehow managed to mask the fact that it was only in the low 50s.

If I had the notion to decline the swim, I would have had the entire tour group staring at me from the shore. So I jumped. And I immediately feared for my life. Never have I been so cold. There are no words to describe the panic and the sensation. I made a beeline for the shore, and as I ran onto the sand, the group was simultaneously laughing and granting me hero status.

As someone wrapped me in a towel, another handed me a shot of vodka, and as I downed it, I could feel the liquid breaking the ice inside my body.

Then the tour leader said that according to custom, anyone who swam in Lake Baikal earned the right to take twenty years off his age. I threw my towel on the ground and raced back into the water. Howls of laughter cheered me from the shore. I took a second shot of vodka but declined the gift of an additional twenty years. I didn't want to be younger than my children.

The guide handed me a certificate that I have to this day. It reads as follows:

Cautioned that the waters of Lake Baikal, the largest fresh water lake in the world, are cold; that dipping into it could as much freeze the body, numb the brains and produce delirium, the person named below took the valourous steps of plunging daringly and swimming into the lake despite the aforesaid warnings.

This certificate is awarded to TED ROBB for the foolhardy and bravado adventure into this unique and singular ritual and by the power bestowed on us by Burkham, the mighty spirit of Lake Baikal, we now pronounce the possessor of this Certificate eternally youthful, with the authority to prune twenty years off his/her age from hereafter. August 17, 2013.

I HAD SUCH FUN TALKING ABOUT THIS SINGULAR EXPERIENCE later at a barbecue hosted by locals in a nearby village in the Baikal hills.

Ted Robb

As we moved along to Moscow, we stopped in Novosibirsk, where we toured the world's largest opera house. We walked through Lenin Square and along the River Ob, which flows 3,500 miles to the Arctic. From there we journeyed to Yekaterinburg, site of the Romanov family's famous execution.

Before I knew it, the Golden Eagle Express had arrived in Moscow. I had last walked in these city streets six decades earlier, taking in Red Square and the Kremlin with Charlie Lord and Sabin Robbins. I doubt I would have envisioned myself returning as an eighty-year-old man.

I recalled memories of that trip and more as I booked a side trip to St. Petersburg aboard a much flashier, faster train. There I hired a guide and enjoyed a wonderful day exploring the city's astounding changes since its post–World War II days.

This trip reestablished the ground that I had so badly lost with Peg's death a year before. I missed her—of course, I did. But the Golden Eagle took me on a train ride through a land that set a new tone for me, proving that life and its risks awaited me in my eighth decade just as they had in my first, when I was a boy of nine, happily following a train conductor around another train, eager to embrace my first adventure far away from home.

Life began again when I stepped onto a train heading west.

⁙ 84 ⁙

When I returned from Siberia, I lived off of my memories of that trip for some time. No matter where I went, when people asked me how I was doing, I had something to talk about other than the death of Peg. Of course, memories of her surrounded me—and they still do. But right after she passed, I only had her death to talk about. Going on such a trip, and taking such a risk, allowed me to see that I had more on my plate to discuss than being a widower. I'm convinced she would have applauded this decision of mine to travel.

My family and I fondly remember how Peg planned vacations around whom we could visit. Even on smaller trips, her modus operandi involved pulling out her book and saying, "We can go here and see…(X, Y, and Z)." I was always complaining about the fact that there was no such thing as a straight line on our journeys. That's one thing that I suppose train rides offer people: a direct route from Point A to Point B!

A fellow travel enthusiast, my friend and Yale classmate Tersh Boasberg, invited me to Washington, DC, to share a talk about my Siberian experience. Tersh's wife died around the same time as Peg, and he also looked to international travel as a way of broadening his horizons as he aged. He asked if I might be interested in taking a trip to Europe with the Yale alumni network, which arranges voyages for graduates to destinations where professors host themed talks.

Soon Tersh and I were planning a voyage to Belgium and France, where we roomed together on a fantastic, sobering trip focused on World War I. I found myself thinking quite a bit about Mal, who was raised in Belgium before becoming a New York City nanny, and also Dad, who had been rescued by Belgians during the war.

Another trip with the same organization led me back to England and the university towns of Oxford and Cambridge. Once again the vacation had a World War I theme, and what I took from it was a much greater awareness of the impact that the Great War had on Great Britain. America entered that war toward its end, and other than Dad's having gone into the service, I had never really given that particular period of international history a whole lot of thought.

One of the great joys of these trips is their emphasis on walking and talking—with others and with oneself—as information is presented and considered. Recent knee and hip replacement operations, unfortunately, have cooled my travel jets. I don't want to go on a trip if I feel like I can't handle the physical challenges. The doctor who performed my last hip replacement told me that I might need another surgery pending certain physical activities, and I don't want to go through that again. This was a real disappointment as I was hoping to get a clean bill of health. As one ages, the fear of taking a perhaps fatal fall tends to loom over certain activities.

I'm not sad, however. Slowly I'm reconciling myself to the fact that I'm not able to operate on a fearless level anymore. The one thing I don't want to surrender is the staircase. If I give up on that, I'm giving up a large measure of independence.

Risk-taking, such as traveling through Siberia, provides a much-needed balance to cautious living. Now that I can't travel like I used to, am I just counting the days of my existence? This project shows that the answer is "no." Writing my memoir has been a much different type of risk. In some ways, traveling through memory and history in search of truth, and then acknowledging and articulating it as such, is a much more rigorous type of adventure.

The pandemic has done a lot to influence my feelings about life in general. I can't be bitter. Because I've been forced to stay indoors at this time in my life, not when I was younger, physically stronger, and professionally more active. Had a crisis come then, I would have been really upset, as so many younger people rightfully are. And, interestingly enough, I've never feared death from COVID-19, as so many older people rightfully have. I've always had the feeling that the pandemic was never going to catch me.

When the time for my departure does come, and all is said and done, I'd like to think there is a Ted Robb footprint on this Earth somewhere. Life has a way of layering our memories on its canvas, and I do wonder how my loved ones will see my portrait when I'm gone. I wonder what colors will appear on it and what details will make the final cut in their minds. Taking refuge in one's memories can be helpful, but it also can be dangerous. It's easy to color our pasts through tinted lenses. I hope I haven't done that too much. I've done my best to present the truth as I see it. It's up to the reader now to take my story and use it to think through their own.

Ted Robb